comfort

comfort

food to soothe the soul

JOHN WHAITE

Photography by Nassima Rothacker

Kyle Books

For my father and
his garlicky cheese on toast

First published in Great Britain in 2017 by
Kyle Books, an imprint of Kyle Cathie Ltd
102–108 Vauxhall Bridge Road
London SW1V 1DX
general.enquiries@kylebooks.com
www.kylebooks.co.uk

10 9 8 7 6 5 4 3 2 1

ISBN 978 0 85783 416 4

Designer: Paul Atkins
Photographer: Nassima Rothacker
Food Stylist: Nicole Herft and John Whaite
Food Stylist Assistants: Rosie MacKean and Holly Cochrane
Props Stylist: Lydia Brun
Project Editor: Sophie Allen
Editorial Assistant: Isabel Gonzalez-Prendergast
Production: Nic Jones, Gemma John and Lisa Pinnell

A Cataloguing in Publication record for this title is available from the British Library.

Colour reproduction by ALTA, London
Printed and bound in China by C&C Offset Printing Co., Ltd.

contents

Introduction

A single black pot is simmering on the stovetop, its lid half-off. Some of the steam escapes, carrying with it a haunting scent of spices, meat and gravy; a ghost dancing through the house. But there's nothing to fear here. I am cosily wrapped in a blanket on the couch, my laptop balanced on top of me; the aroma lulls me into a light sleep. The only thing to jolt me awake is the same steam, condensing on the pan lid and dripping into the flame with a sharp sizzle.

It's early autumn but it feels far later in the year. The leaf-littered world outside has commanded our downtime: go inside and close the doors; light the fires; nestle down and take stock. I am alone, entirely, but I do not feel alone. Paul, my partner, won't be home for four more hours, but I am calm. I am bolstered by the broth, simmering on my stovetop.

A sudden cinnamon scent wafts by; another spectre appears. I'm seven again, and have just moved into Robin Hood Farm – an ancient barn, with exposed beams and creaky floors – in Lancashire. It's Christmastime, but the feeling isn't the same as in previous years. There's something eerie about this house, which makes the protective familiarity of Christmas even more poignant. My mother has softened the old building with boughs of pine, holly and ivy, which snake all the way up the bannister rail. Pinecones, raffia and dried orange slices shyly peek out from amongst the needles and leaves. A cinnamon stick catches my eye. I pluck it from the bough and instantly regret doing so: the scent has been artificially amplified. As with potpourri, a single waft is quaint; a deep sniff is startling. The smell will stain my hands for hours; cinnamon will always confuse me.

The power of food and ingredients is magic. They can somehow flick a single switch and ignite a roaring furnace of memory. It can even be necromantic; with a single sniff of a punnet of cherry tomatoes, a lost aunt is brought back to life. Vivid pictures of her outfits and the words she used

reappear in my mind. It's hard to say whether I have manufactured certain aspects of the memory, but the essence, the raw feeling about her, is undoubtedly real.

It's down to science, of course – most illusions are. Our olfactory bulbs are linked directly to the areas of the brain where memories are processed. With a fleeting scent or mere morsel, a part of our personal history can re-enact itself. Science it may be, but it still feels like magic.

We've come to use that power of involuntary memory to our advantage; we call it comfort food. If you've had a bad day; a moment of stress at work; some awful news that rears its ugly head out of the blue and blindsides you, you may very well reach for something soothing. Some research suggests that those with stronger emotional ties will claw for comfort food when emotionally burdened. That makes sense; food can be the conduit to people or situations with whom, or in which, we feel, quite simply, safe.

Another research study shunned the belief in comfort food. It concludes that any food – even a bag of nuts – will have the same easing effect as something hearty or familiar. I don't hold with that opinion. That's ignorant of me, yes, but I choose to believe that, while the after-effects of comfort eating may be the same regardless of the food you consume (I don't believe that, either) the initial comfort is incomparable. It may be some drastic flaw in my willpower, some irreparable weakness in me, but when someone or something does me an injustice the idea of warm carbs or melted cheese is more appealing and far more urgent than a carrot stick and cold hummus.

It isn't a matter of stuffing as much junk into your mouth as possible: particular foods and the way they are cooked form an identity, both individual and cultural. Food, and comfort food in particular, is autobiographically relevant. People want to belong, and what we eat links us to, if not serves to define, that identity.

That said, the urgent longings we have for comfort food don't always command a single or particular dish. I think we are all familiar with that rapacious pursuit for something tender or sticky, or something gooey and molten; it's sometimes the characteristics of comfort food and the textures that first impel us. We might not know precisely what we want, but we can be damn sure of what we are in the mood for. I know when I am poorly, I want something I can eat from a bowl with a spoon, while I'm snuggled on the couch and tucked under my duvet. And when I'm hungover? Well, it's got to be something crunchy or cheesy, and full of carbs that I want, probably even before I've woken. That's why I've based each chapter in this book around a property of comfort food.

Some of these dishes are deeply personal to me; others are recipes I have created to share. This book is a bit of a mongrel, there's no cultural theme here (other than my Lancastrian roots), and I hope I can introduce you to something new, but as equally comforting as the food you've grown to love.

Food for the body is not enough.

There must be food for the soul.

Dorothy Day

A Final Note: Keen Eating
I intended this book to be a rebellion against the current trend of Clean Eating – a trend that has bewitched people's view of food. But, as is the case with comfort food, experimenting with these flavours and writing these recipes saw so many of my own memories float to the surface. It seemed wrong to reinter these flickers from my past just to undermine a heavily marketed food fad. The food across these pages doesn't need to be shouted from the rooftops – this food is very much already known. It lifts us when we feel blue; it's the hug we crave from a lost love. This food has always been, and always will be, a part of who we are. The lycra-clad clan of self-flagellation is only fooling itself.

something cheesy

The Cheese Years

Among my friends, the most peculiar are the ones who don't like cheese. Unless they have some dietary requirement, forcing them to avoid even a mild Cheddar, I don't understand the words 'I don't like cheese'.

For me cheese has landmarked my life, as I am sure will be the case for many. As a child, mild to medium Cheddar was just about manageable. Do you remember the slight rubbery texture, as you'd bite down into a chunk of yellow Cheddar then pull away to inspect the perfect tooth marks? My uncle Karl once found this to be sufficiently incriminating evidence against my cousin Tom, who had nibbled the corner of a slab. Like a police line-up, Tom and I stood, backs to the wall, while Karl asked us to flash our pearly whites. He held the cheese to our teeth, inspecting the jigsaw with angst-inducing delay – enough to scare the crap out of us, and make me question my own innocence. The circumstantial evidence proved unfavourable for Tom; though both condemned and acquitted enjoyed a slice on a digestive with the judiciary once the case was closed.

My interest beyond the breezeblocks of Cheddar and the slices of 'plastic cheese' was ignited by my dad when he took me to Chorley market for a piece of Creamy Lancashire. All I can remember, quite vividly, is an arm stemming from a dark market stall, holding a knife – the dagger before me – balancing upon which was a shaving of the cheese. My dad plucked it from the blade and popped it straight into my mouth. Strong, meaty and smooth, this would become a favourite for life. My sister and I used to enjoy bowls of cubed Creamy Lancashire and apples, eaten together on the sofa.

My early teens – the Stilton years – were spent experimenting with the questionable fruit-filled cheeses, and perhaps the odd reputable blue, but it was only as I really matured that my palate caught up. My first taste of something pungent was a chunk of Stinking Bishop – a Gloucestershire semi-soft, washed in perry as it ages. Although the smell was something I could barely abide, it intrigued me enough to taste. My head spun as the nasal tanginess transformed to silky creaminess. From then on I was Pac Man in the supermarket, munching samples, begging for tasters, pleading for hunks of Roquefort and wheels of Brie de Meaux or a more complex-tasting Epoisses.

The Cheeseboard

Creating an impressive cheeseboard is simple. Just pick four or five cheeses of contrasting strengths and textures, and arrange with other bits and bobs. The cheeseboard I always assemble, whether for students at my cookery school or my friends on a Friday night, rarely changes. I may add the occasional special guest cheese, but the main cast remains unchanged.

The cheeses I always opt for are:

St Agur or Roquefort
Both are fairly strong and salty blues, but the St Agur is a touch softer and finer than the rugged, punchy Roquefort. Normally I'd opt for the Roquefort, but I do have an incurable weakness for St Agur.

Creamy Lancashire
This is a firm cheese, but with a fluffy, slightly crumbly creaminess. Its flavour is nutty and meaty. It makes for the best cheese on toast, especially if you rub the toasted bread with a cut garlic clove before adding the cheese and melting – a speciality from my dad that I enjoyed in my childhood.

Epoisses de Bourgogne
This pasty cow's milk cheese is so soft that if served on warm days, it is best scooped up with a spoon. It is washed in brandy as it matures, and its taste is strong, slightly salty, earthy and nutty. It's pungent and complex, for sure, and one of my all-time favourites.

Chaource
In its softness this is similar to Brie and Epoisses, but not at all soft enough to scoop up with a spoon. I find this to be the cheese with the split personality in both texture and flavour: it has an outer creaminess, then a firmer, mealy inside. Its flavour is soft, gentle and creamy, but beneath that stillness lurks a raw tanginess.

These are all cow's milk cheeses, so sometimes I'll add a slice of British Rosary goat's cheese, which isn't overly strong, but has a welcome acidic creaminess.

When it comes to accompaniments, I like to go perhaps a little too far. Small, perfumed figs are a must, as are radishes and cornichon gherkins, which supply their sharpness to cut through all of that cream. Nuts are essential: sometimes pecans, sometimes walnuts, but mostly I like the sweet, toasted almond-extract flavour of Marcona almonds. And if my cheeseboard doesn't contain charcuterie, I'm not happy; I like prosciutto, bresaola and a peppery sausage-style slice. Baby Gem lettuce, black grapes and pear slices add colour, texture and refreshing variety. Sometimes I'll serve great hunks of sourdough, or sometimes crackers – I like the Peter's Yard selection box: the charcoal and rye sourdough crispbreads are the best.

Assembling the Cheeseboard

I have a huge wooden board with deep sides that you could say I stole (I prefer to say rescued) from my parents. They found it at some antiques market and had it propped up against the wall in the kitchen, never used.

The almonds, olives, cornichons and crackers I put into individual pots and dot those on the board. The temptation is to do this symmetrically but that looks naff, so go against any impulses for evenness. I then slice the Baby Gems in half along the length, and put them here and there, then I add the cheeses. Any larger gaps can be filled in with enticing bundles of the charcuterie. To finish the masterpiece, everything is brought together with the purples and blacks of the figs, radishes and grapes. Slices of pear finish it all off beautifully.

something cheesy

Onion Soup with an Epoisses & Caraway Crust

There are many different ways of making a French onion soup: some recipes involve wine, some cognac, while others use both. I'm supposing that most regions of France, if not most families, will have their own method and ingredients list. Epoisses is a cheese from Burgundy and I haven't seen it used for the characteristically lavish crust, but for me it's a no-brainer: the cheese is soft and pungent, accompanying the sweet onions perfectly. Here I've rounded out the Epoisses with some Comté. Caraway is something I eat regularly with Epoisses — if not caraway bread I just scatter the seeds over spoonfuls of the cheese.

I find the sweetness of pink onions — Roscoff or Rosanna — makes for the best soup, but if they prove a little trickier to come by, just use half red and half brown.

Preheat the oven to 200°C/180°C fan/gas mark 6.

For the croûtons, place the torn baguette onto a baking sheet and toss together with the garlic oil and caraway seeds. Bake for 5–10 minutes, or until dry and crispy.

For the soup, heat the olive oil and butter in a large saucepan or casserole over a high heat. When the butter melts, add the onions and cook for 10 minutes or so, until they are starting to colour around the edges. Once they are gently browned, reduce the heat to low and cook slowly for anything up to 40 minutes. The onions should caramelise deeply, and smell strong and sweet.

When the onions are caramelised, add the flour and stir to coat the onions. Increase the heat to high, wait a minute for the pan to get hot, then pour in the wine and let it bubble and evaporate almost entirely. Add the stock and bring to the boil, then reduce to a simmer and cook for 45 minutes, partially covered. Stir in the chutney, if using, and salt and pepper to taste.

Preheat the grill.

Divide the soup between serving bowls — make sure they're heatproof — then scatter over the croûtons. Slice the Epoisses into fairly thin slices (do so quickly before it starts to melt) and lay them on top of the croûtons. Scatter over the Comté and grill until the cheese has melted and burned a little at the edges.

SERVES 2–4

For the croûtons
1 x French baguette,
  torn into chunks
1 tbsp garlic oil
  (or olive oil, if you prefer)
1 tbsp caraway seeds
150g Epoisses
  cheese, chilled
100g Comté cheese,
  coarsely grated

For the soup
1 tbsp olive oil
100g unsalted butter
500g pink onions,
  finely sliced
2 tbsp plain flour
175ml dry white wine
1 litre beef stock
1 tbsp onion chutney
  (optional, but
  damn good)
Fine sea salt and coarsely
  ground black pepper

something cheesy

Pea Soup with Parmesan Pretzel Crust

I'm unashamed to use frozen peas. Some chefs may turn their nose up at them, but I am not fussy. Especially not when they enable such a bowlful of comfort within the hour. The idea of this soup is to marry the classic combination of peas and Parmesan, with the incredibly comforting form of a French onion soup, topped with cheesy croûtons. The pretzel top came about when I was enjoying a bag of pretzels after my fish-and-chips supper (I know, carbo-cide). Without thinking I dipped a pretzel into my leftover peas – it was love at first bite. I tried making this both with the small pretzel snacks and with pretzel bread. Both versions were gorgeous, but I much preferred it with the doughiness of the bread; the crisps turned too soggy too quickly.

SERVES 4–6

For the soup

50g unsalted butter
2 onions,
 roughly chopped
1 large potato, diced
2 thyme sprigs
2 garlic cloves,
 lightly crushed
750g frozen peas,
 defrosted
1 litre chicken or
 vegetable stock
2 tbsp soured cream
Fine sea salt and
 coarsely ground
 black pepper

For the topping

200g pretzel bread,
 torn into small chunks
Olive oil, to drizzle
200g Parmesan,
 coarsely grated
100g mozzarella,
 shredded

Heat a large saucepan or casserole over a high heat and add the butter. As soon as it melts add the onions, potato and thyme, reduce the heat to medium and cook for 15 minutes or so, stirring frequently, until the potatoes are just starting to soften. Add the garlic to the pan and stir until fragrant, then add the peas and stock. Bring to the boil, then reduce to a simmer and cook for 20 minutes.

Preheat the oven to 200°C/180°C fan/gas mark 6.

For the topping, scatter the chunks of pretzel onto a baking sheet and drizzle with a little olive oil. Bake for 10 minutes, or until crisp.

Preheat the grill.

Once the soup is cooked, add the soured cream, and use a hand-held immersion blender or a food processor to blitz smooth. Portion the soup into heatproof bowls, top with a handful of pretzel croûtons and the mixed cheeses, and grill until the cheese melts and starts to blister. Serve immediately.

Caramelised Shallot, Honey & Roquefort Cornbread

Cornbread, for me, conjures romantic images of the Deep South. I imagine an incredibly close day, with beads of condensation slipping down the side of my cocktail – probably a Mint Julep or an Old Fashioned. But that fantasy will dissolve instantly when I tell you that this version of cornbread couldn't be further from the authentic recipe from America's southern states. Roquefort and shallots are the obvious diversion. This would be considered a northern cornbread; not only is the use of wheat flour definitely from northern persuasion, but also the use of fine cornmeal would be frowned upon (or shot at) in the South. It's a risk I'm willing to take.

Preheat the oven to 200°C/180°C fan/gas mark 6. Grease a 23cm round cake tin (preferably not loose-bottom) and line with baking paper.

Peel the shallots, halve lengthways and place them into the tin, sliced-side downwards, with the thyme leaves, honey, oil and a good pinch of salt and pepper. Toss everything together, then roast the shallots for 25–30 minutes, until soft and lightly coloured. Remove the tin from the oven and allow to cool slightly.

Pull the Roquefort into small chunks and dot these in and amongst the shallots.

For the cornbread, sift the cornmeal, flour, baking powder, sugar and 1 teaspoon salt into a mixing bowl. Beat together the eggs, buttermilk and melted butter in a jug, then fold the mixture into the dry ingredients – I use a balloon whisk – until you have a smooth batter. Pour the batter carefully over the shallots, level out, then bake for 20–25 minutes, until a skewer inserted into the centre comes out clean.

Meanwhile, melt the butter in a pan with the honey.

When the cornbread is baked, allow to cool in the tin for 5 minutes, then invert onto a plate and peel off the baking paper. Pour the butter-honey mixture over the top and allow it to soak into the cornbread.

This is best served warm.

SERVES 8–10

For the shallot topping

8 banana shallots

Leaves from 3
   thyme sprigs

2 tbsp runny honey

1 tbsp sunflower oil

100g Roquefort

Fine sea salt and coarsely
   ground black pepper

For the cornbread

140g fine cornmeal

140g self-raising flour

1 tsp baking powder

50g light brown sugar

2 large eggs

300ml buttermilk

30g unsalted
   butter, melted

To finish

50g unsalted butter

2 tbsp honey

Artichoke & Mushroom Lasagne

When I was last in New York, I was lucky enough to get a table at I Sodi, a small Italian restaurant in West Village serving awesome cocktails and rustic Tuscan fare. There I had the most delicious vegetarian lasagne I have ever tasted (I exaggerate not). Layer upon layer of al dente pasta with an oozing cheese and artichoke sauce, spiked gently with fresh nutmeg. I couldn't pluck up the courage to ask for the recipe, so I've tried to work it out for myself, and this isn't too far off. Nutmeg is such a haunting spice; it's a ghostly reminder of the white sauces and rice puddings from my childhood. I can't recommend enough that you use fresh nutmeg and finely grate it yourself; the ready-ground nutmeg seems to have such a mouth-numbing, almost ferric, flavour. Fresh is best.

SERVES 6–8

3 tbsp olive oil
1 small onion,
  finely chopped
500g chestnut
  mushrooms,
  very finely chopped
  (I use a food processor)
500g fresh
  lasagne sheets

For the sauce
125g unsalted butter,
  plus extra for greasing
125g plain flour
1 litre milk
500ml vegetable stock
200g (drained weight)
  artichoke hearts from
  a jar, finely chopped
1½ tsp finely chopped
  fresh rosemary
1½ tsp freshly
  grated nutmeg
1 tsp fine sea salt
1 tsp freshly ground
  black pepper
350g Gruyère, plus
  a little extra for the
  top, finely grated
2 tbsp vodka
  (or white wine)

Heat a large frying pan over a high heat and add the olive oil. Once the oil is hot add the onions and mushrooms with a pinch of salt and pepper, and fry, stirring very frequently, for a good 5 minutes, until softened and fairly dry – the aim here is to try to remove as much moisture as possible from the onions and mushrooms, and cooking them at a high heat will do that quickly, if they are stirred (otherwise they'll burn). Remove from the heat.

For the sauce, put the butter into a medium-large saucepan over a medium-high heat and allow it to melt, stirring occasionally. As soon as the butter has melted, add the flour and beat vigorously with a wooden spoon until everything comes together into a very thick paste. Allow this paste to cook for a minute just until it turns a touch darker, then slowly add the milk, beating frequently after each drop. The mixture will seem to get even thicker at first, but this is normal – don't panic.

As the milk is absorbed, you can start to add the stock in the same way. By this point, I find it useful to switch to a whisk to ensure the sauce is very well mixed. Allow the sauce to bubble for a minute or two. Add the chopped artichokes, rosemary, nutmeg, salt, pepper, cheese and vodka. Reduce the heat to low and stir for 3–4 minutes. The sauce should be as thick as double cream and as smooth as possible. Remove from the heat and set aside until needed.

Stir the cooked mushrooms and onion into the sauce.

Preheat the oven to 200°C/180°C fan/gas mark 6. Grease a 20cm square cake tin (not loose-bottom) with butter, then line the base with lasagne sheets, trimming them to size if necessary.

Pour over just enough of the sauce to cover the pasta, then repeat the layers until all the sauce and pasta are used, but do make sure that the last layer is sauce and not pasta. Sprinkle over a little extra Gruyère and bake for 50–60 minutes, or until the sauce is bubbling and the top is very deeply bronzed, perhaps crispy. Remove from the oven and allow to rest for 10 minutes before serving.

Marmite & Cheddar Welsh Rarebit

I recently ate at Pedler in Peckham Rye, southeast London, a dimly lit restaurant serving a selection of awesome small plates. My favourite was roasted sweet potato with Marmite and Cheddar béchamel. That startling strong sauce was so good that I ordered a bowlful with chips for dipping. A day later I found myself stirring a potful of the sauce in my own kitchen, to slather, liberally, over toast. This recipe was born.

Preheat the grill to high. Toast the slices of sourdough, either under the grill or in the toaster; toast is toast.

Put the butter in a small saucepan over a medium-high heat. Once the butter has completely melted, add the flour and beat to a thick paste with a wooden spoon. Still on the heat, add a splash of the ale and beat in. The mixture will turn to a very thick paste, but just keep beating. Add the ale gradually, beating well after each addition. As the mixture gets looser, switch to a whisk and whisk continuously, while pouring in the ale – it's easier to get rid of any lumps while the mixture is thicker, so whisk like your life depends on it and add the ale gradually. Allow the sauce to come to the boil then reduce to a gentle simmer, and leave it to cook for about 10 minutes, stirring occasionally.

Once the floury taste has cooked out of the sauce – test it to be sure – add a generous pinch of black pepper (I wouldn't add any salt until the end as the Marmite can season this enough). Add the cheese and stir over a low heat until melted. Add the Marmite a little at a time, to taste – you may think more is more, but please go carefully: a little goes a long way. Taste for seasoning, adding more pepper and salt if required.

Spoon the sauce onto the slices of toast and sprinkle over a little more grated cheese. Place under the hot grill for a minute or two, until the sauce bubbles up and burnished, blackened little flecks appear.

MAKES 4 SLICES

4 slices of sourdough
20g unsalted butter
20g plain flour
200ml amber ale
100g mature Cheddar, finely grated, plus extra for sprinkling
1–2 tsp Marmite, to taste
Sea salt flakes and coarsely ground black pepper

Tartiflette Pizza

When you put carbs onto carbs, you just know the result is going to be a successful one. And when you throw cheese and cream into the works, well, that combination just speaks for itself. I've only once seen, and indeed tried, tartiflette pizza. It was my birthday and my partner and I found ourselves in Castellane, not far from Nice in the south of France. We had driven through the mountains from Nice to find a place to white-water raft. In this quiet little town we sat outside an empty restaurant, warmed by an electric heater, and devoured two of these. Tartiflette is a hearty potato dish from the Savoy region made with the local cheese, Reblochon, and is designed, no doubt, to keep out the cold. Served as a pizza topping, it is comfort food at its best.

SERVES 1–2

For the dough

200g strong white
    bread flour
7g sachet fast-
    action yeast
1 tsp fine sea salt
140ml warm water

For the tartiflette

2 tbsp sunflower oil
200g smoked
    streaky bacon,
    roughly chopped
1 small onion,
    very finely sliced
50g unsalted butter
350g Charlotte
    potatoes, cut
    into 1cm cubes
3 garlic cloves,
    unpeeled
150ml dry white wine
150ml double cream
240g Reblochon cheese
Fine sea salt and
    coarsely ground
    black pepper

For the dough, simply combine the ingredients in a large bowl and mix until everything comes together to form a scraggy mass. Knead the dough either by hand for about 10 minutes or in a mixer fitted with a dough hook for 5 minutes. It's absolutely crucial that you don't add any more flour. This dough will be quite wet, and that is precisely right. Not a single grain more! As soon as the dough is smooth and elastic, it is ready. Put the dough into a greased bowl and cover with cling film. Leave to rest until doubled in size.

Meanwhile, make the tartiflette. Heat a large frying pan over a high heat and once it is hot add 1 tablespoon of the sunflower oil and the bacon and onion. Reduce the heat to medium and cook until the bacon is fairly crispy and the onion is soft and a little browned. Tip into a bowl and set aside until needed.

Return the pan to a medium heat and add the remaining tablespoon of oil along with the butter. Add the potatoes and garlic cloves to the pan and leave to cook slowly for about 25–30 minutes, tossing the pan occasionally. This may seem like a long time, but it's better to cook the potatoes over a lower heat for longer, to achieve an unrivalled inner tenderness and outer crispiness. Once the potatoes are cooked, turn the heat to high and add the wine, allowing it to bubble and evaporate completely. Add the cream and cook it until thickly reduced – don't worry if it splits. Stir in 1 teaspoon each of salt and pepper, remove and discard the garlic cloves, then remove the pan from the heat and add the tartiflette to the bowl with the bacon and onion. Roughly chop half of the cheese and add it to the bowl.

Preheat the oven to 250°C/230°C fan/gas mark 9 and place a baking sheet or pizza stone into the oven to get hot.

Once the dough has doubled in size, dust a second baking sheet liberally with flour and roll out the dough to a disc about 23cm in diameter. Check the disc of dough isn't stuck down to the baking sheet – give the sheet a quick jerk back and forward to ensure the disc moves freely on the flour. Scatter the tartiflette mixture over the dough, slice the remaining cheese and add that, then slide the pizza off the cold baking sheet and onto the hot one in the oven. Bake for 7–10 minutes until the edge of the pizza is puffed up and golden. Serve immediately.

Crab & Sriracha Mac 'n' Cheese

Macaroni cheese has to be up there with my favourite comfort foods – out of the four books I have written so far, three contain a recipe for mac 'n' cheese. I think it stems from childhood and the pasta bakes mum used to make for us – I only ever once ate the canned variety and remember the results (not of an appropriate nature to write about descriptively here). This version is for more mature palates, as it's enriched with crabmeat and spiced with mustard, Asian chilli sauce and cayenne. It is based on a lobster mac 'n' cheese I had at Beauty & Essex in Manhattan a few years ago.

Cook the macaroni according to the packet instructions, then drain and set aside.

Preheat the oven to 200°C/180°C fan/gas mark 6.

Heat the butter in a large saucepan over a medium-high heat until the butter melts, then stir in the flour using a wooden spoon to make a very thick paste. Allow the paste to cook for a minute until browned slightly, then beat in a ladleful of milk – it will get quickly absorbed, so repeat. When you've added all the milk, switch to a whisk and add the stock, a little at a time, whisking to avoid any lumps. As soon as the liquids are incorporated, add the cheeses, reserving a little to sprinkle on top, along with the mustard, sriracha and cayenne pepper. Reduce the heat to a simmer for 10 minutes, then season to taste, remembering that when you add the pasta the seasoning will be diluted, so over-season.

Add the crabmeat, parsley and macaroni to the sauce to combine well and tip into a medium-sized roasting dish. Sprinkle over the reserved cheese and the breadcrumbs and bake for 25–30 minutes until hot and bubbling.

SERVES 6

400g macaroni
100g butter
100g plain flour
500ml milk
500ml chicken stock
150g Gruyère,
    finely grated
150g strong Cheddar,
    finely grated
1 tbsp wholegrain
    mustard
6 tbsp sriracha sauce,
    plus extra to serve
1 tsp cayenne pepper
300g white crabmeat
2 tbsp chopped flat-
    leaf parsley
25g breadcrumbs
Fine sea salt and freshly
    ground black pepper

Pear, Gorgonzola & Walnut Risotto

As with so much Italian food, risottos are unduly shrouded in rules and regulations. Naturally, there are specific processes that should be followed (hot stock, stirring…) but I think we Brits sometimes overestimate the orders. The process really is a simple one: get the rice cooked, well flavoured, and you'll have a dish to behold. Some risottos are cooked to be creamy so that they flow on the plate while some will be thick enough to stand a spoon up in. This is a creamier version, achieved by using carnaroli rice (which is more forgiving and holds its shape better than arborio) and 'la mantecatura' (a vigorous stirring toward the end of cooking).

SERVES 4

For the pickled pear

2 tbsp white
  wine vinegar

2 tsp caster sugar

½ Comice pear, peeled,
  cored and finely diced

For the risotto

100g walnuts,
  roughly chopped

1 tbsp olive oil

90g unsalted butter

2 banana shallots,
  very finely chopped

2 celery sticks,
  finely diced

½ Comice pear, peeled,
  cored and finely diced

300g carnaroli rice

175ml dry white wine

1.5 litres hot chicken
  or vegetable stock

200g Gorgonzola, torn
  into rough chunks

Small handful of rocket

Fine sea salt and freshly
  ground black pepper

To pickle the pear, simply stir together the vinegar and sugar until the sugar has dissolved, then add the pear cubes. Set aside at room temperature until the risotto is ready.

Heat a sauté or deep-sided frying pan over a high heat. Once the pan is hot, add the walnuts and toast them, tossing the pan occasionally, for 1–2 minutes, just until you can smell their rich nuttiness. Pour the walnuts into a small bowl and set aside until needed.

Put the oil and 50g of the butter into the same pan and, as soon as the butter melts, add the shallots, celery and pear, and reduce the heat to medium. Cook, stirring occasionally, until the onion and celery have softened – at least 20 minutes.

Increase the heat to medium-high and add the rice to the pan, stirring to coat it in the oil. Add the wine and allow it to bubble until almost entirely absorbed or evaporated, then add a ladleful of the hot stock and allow that to be absorbed, stirring frequently. Repeat the process, a ladleful of hot stock at a time, until all the stock is used and the rice is just cooked through – if you run out of stock before the rice is cooked, use hot water. And don't let the rice stick to the bottom of the pan and become crispy.

Once the risotto is cooked, remove the pan from the heat and stir in the Gorgonzola and remaining butter. Stir it vigorously for a good minute to help make the sauce as creamy and smooth as possible (*la mantecatura*). Add the rocket and allow it to wilt into the risotto, then season to taste – I like a lot of salt and pepper here, but seasoning is always down to personal preference. Garnish with the toasted walnuts and pickled pear.

Lancashire Aligot &
Cumbrian Sausage

You may think that this is just bangers and mash, but it's so much more than that. Aligot is a French potato dish, similar to mashed potatoes, but richly spiked with garlic, cream and melted cheese. Traditionally it's made with a mountain cheese like Cantal or Tomme, but that's scarcely available in the UK, so I've gone back to my roots and used a tasty Lancashire. I also infuse the cream first with bay and garlic, and I finish it off with nutmeg – this isn't traditional either, but this is, of course, my own version.

Preheat the oven to 200°C/180°C fan/gas mark 6.

Put the cream into a saucepan with the bay leaves and garlic and bring to a boil, then switch off the heat and leave the cream to infuse.

Put the potatoes into a saucepan of well-salted water, ensuring the water covers the potatoes by a good 2cm, then bring to the boil. Boil the potatoes for 15–20 minutes, until a knife pierces them easily, and drain.

Meanwhile, put the sausages into a roasting dish and roast for 20–25 minutes, until cooked through and coloured.

Press the warm potatoes through a potato ricer back into the dry pan, and set the pan over a low-medium heat. Stirring constantly with a wooden spoon – this is where elbow grease is required – cook the potatoes for just a minute or two, then beat in the butter a little at a time. Remove the bay and garlic from the cream and pour it into the potatoes, beating constantly. Once the cream is fully incorporated, add the cheese and stir vigorously – the aligot will give as good as it gets, but keep going until it's fairly smooth and runs from the spoon like thick, melted cheese. Season the aligot with salt and pepper and stir in the nutmeg to taste.

Serve bowlfuls of aligot with sausages for dunking.

SERVES 4

250ml single cream
2 bay leaves
2 garlic cloves, peeled but left whole
500g new potatoes
8 large, fat Cumbrian sausages (not the curly kind)
125g unsalted butter, cold and cubed
250g Tasty/Creamy Lancashire cheese
Freshly grated nutmeg, to taste
Fine sea salt and freshly ground black pepper

Spanish Beef Mince & Cauliflower Cheese

You'd be forgiven for thinking me unpatriotic to take a British classic and give it a Spanish heartbeat, but I march into Spain with the Union Jack held high. This takes the classic side dish a few steps further, by including broccoli as well as cauliflower, and transforms it into a meal in its own right: beneath that fluffy and cheesy topping lurks a bold combination of minced beef and chorizo.

Set a large saucepan or casserole over a medium heat and pour in the oil. Once it is hot, add the onion and chorizo and cook until the onion is soft and coated in the paprika-spiked oil from the chorizo. Add the smoked paprika and garlic and fry for a minute, then add the lemon juice, beef stock, mince and chickpeas. Bring the mixture to the boil, then reduce to a simmer and cook for 1 hour, uncovered. After this time, turn off the heat and stir in the parsley, along with a generous pinch of salt and pepper. Set aside until needed.

Preheat the oven to 200°C/180°C fan/gas mark 6.

Arrange the broccoli and cauliflower florets, well spaced, on a baking sheet and roast for 25–30 minutes, just until slightly dry-looking and a little charred.

Meanwhile, heat a saucepan over a high heat and add the butter. As soon as the butter melts and starts to sputter, add the flour and stir in to form a thick paste. Add the milk, a little at a time, stirring well after each addition to ensure no lumps form. When all of the milk is added, allow the mixture to come to the boil – don't stop stirring – then add the cheese and reduce the heat to low. Allow the cheese to melt into the sauce.

When the broccoli and cauliflower have roasted, put them into a bowl and stir in the cheese sauce.

Transfer the minced beef to a medium-sized baking dish and top with the cauliflower cheese. Bake for 50–60 minutes, until the top is golden brown, and the sauce beneath is piping hot.

SERVES 6

For the minced beef
2 tbsp olive oil
1 large onion, finely sliced
200g smoked chorizo,
    finely sliced
½ tsp smoked paprika
3 garlic cloves,
    peeled and sliced
Juice of ½ lemon
500ml beef stock
500g minced beef
400g can chickpeas,
    drained
Small handful of
    flat-leaf parsley,
    roughly chopped
Fine sea salt and coarsely
    ground black pepper

For the cauliflower cheese
1kg mixed broccoli and
    cauliflower florets
50g unsalted butter
50g plain flour
600ml whole milk
400g Manchego,
    coarsely grated

something spicy

A Little Kick

There's an irksome bravado that can surround spices in our western culture. Some folk use them as a tool for horseplay, a conveyor of strength and endurance. Blokes in Indian takeaways, slumped beside pints of ice-cold lager, order the hottest curries on the menu. Cheered on by their pals, spoonfuls of fire are shovelled into mouths in-between masculine war cries, masking yelps of pain. Sweat beads are wiped from brows; pure white tablecloths are dirtied in the process.

There's nothing wrong with all of this, I guess – I love a mightily spicy curry every once in a while, and have myself wiped away drips of perspiration to the rhythm of masculine chant – but real spices, beyond the ferocious heat of chillies, form a gentler, more elegant subject. Picture three or four cardamom pods floating in a saucepan of steaming milk; it's almost angelic. Sipped quietly from a mug, while I'm wrapped in a dressing gown on the sofa before bed, this kind of spice is calming – and definitely something I would recommend.

Spicing is an art form – alchemy, perhaps. Like relationships, spices differ in their characters. Some dishes long to be fuelled by the passionate heat of chilli – my Chicken, Apricot and Scotch Bonnet Jollof (see page 54) for example, relies on that sweet kick from the Scotch Bonnets. Others, like my Spiced Chicken in Milk (see page 53), have a softer, more reassuring, profile. But however you prefer to get your kicks, your spices must be treated properly.

Treating Spices Right

As jazzy as your worktop spice rack may be, and as proud of it you may find yourself, it's pretty useless unless sheltered somewhere in a darkened corner. Spices must be kept - for longer periods of time, at least - in darkened, cool, dry areas.

Many books recommend rotating stock every six months. I get through spices like a madman. I have used some from my mum's cupboard 3 years or so past their use-by-date, and they were awful: fresh is a must. Whole spices that are on the verge of losing their oomphf – seeds and sticks – can be easily revived with a brief stint in a hot pan or oven.

The use of salt in spicing is essential. Seasoning is always personal, but an extra grain or two, beyond your usual comfort zone, will make a world of difference.

Aubergine & Feta Chilaquiles

Sod's law is a bugger. It was only on the final day of my last trip to Brooklyn that I decided to eat at Reynard, the restaurant at the Wythe Hotel. Had I been sooner, I'd have eaten every brunch in there. The service was impeccable and the food matched that standard. I had this for brunch and, although not a traditional manifestation of the Mexican chilaquiles, it was absolutely what I needed after a week of sugar, beer and deep-fried food.

SERVES 2

Olive oil, for frying
1 wheat tortilla,
    cut into 8 slices

For the salsa
1 red onion,
    finely chopped
1 aubergine, finely diced
2 garlic cloves, minced
1 tsp ground cumin
1 tsp chilli powder
½ tsp dried oregano
400g can chopped
    tomatoes
100ml water
Fine sea salt and freshly
    ground black pepper

For the eggs
30g unsalted butter
2 large eggs

To serve
50g feta
1 spring onion,
    finely sliced
Lime wedges

To crisp up the tortilla, heat a tablespoon or so of olive oil in a frying pan over a high heat. Once the oil is hot, add the tortilla slices and fry for 1–2 minutes per side, until crispy. Transfer to a plate lined with kitchen paper to cool.

To make the salsa, fry the onion and aubergine in a glug of oil in the same frying pan over a medium-high heat, stirring frequently, until softened and golden. Stir in the garlic, spices and oregano, then add the tomatoes. Stir-fry until the tomatoes are very mushy. Add the water, bring the mixture to the boil and reduce the heat to a simmer for 10 minutes. Season to taste.

Have two plates ready before you fry the eggs. Divide the crispy tortilla slices between the plates and top with the salsa.

To fry the eggs, heat a frying pan over a medium-high heat and add the butter with a drop of olive oil. Once the butter has melted and starts to sizzle, crack in the eggs and fry until the whites set. Cover the pan with a lid or large plate and cook just until the yolks cloud over.

Place an egg on top of each plated serving and crumble over the feta. Finish with a scattering of spring onion and lime wedges for squeezing.

Tarka Dhal

Dhal is a doubly comforting dish: it has that reassuring sloppiness of mushy peas or mashed potatoes, yet still packs a fulfilling punch with its slightly muted spiciness. That flavour is thanks to the tarka – a blend of spices is cooked separately in oil (and butter, in my case), then added to the cooked lentils. If you can get fresh curry leaves for this recipe, it will be so much better. They're stronger and impart their unique flavour – for me their flavour is more of a feeling: something in between a pop and a click in the mouth.

Put the lentils into a sieve and run under cold water until the water draining from the lentils runs clear. Add the lentils to a pan with the turmeric and stock (or water) and bring to the boil. Once the liquid is boiling, reduce the heat to a brisk simmer and cook for about 30 minutes, until the lentils are very tender. Turn off the heat and leave the lentils for a good 15 minutes to plump up even more.

For the tarka, put the vegetable oil and butter into a frying pan over a high heat. As soon the butter melts add the mustard, cumin and nigella seeds, along with the bay leaf and curry leaves. Fry for a few minutes, until the spices smell strongly aromatic, then add the chilli and onion. Reduce the heat to medium and fry, stirring frequently, until the onion is soft and just lightly golden – about 15 minutes. Add the garlic, ginger and tomato and increase the heat to medium-high. Cook until the tomato breaks down and, once the oil has risen to the surface, the tarka is ready.

Stir the lentils vigorously to break them down, then add the tarka. Return to the heat to warm through, season to taste, garnish with the chopped coriander and serve with the rotis or chapatis.

SERVES 2

160g red split lentils
1 tsp ground turmeric
500ml vegetable
   stock or water

For the tarka
1 tbsp vegetable oil
50g unsalted butter
1 tsp black mustard seeds
2 tsp cumin seeds
1 tsp nigella seeds
1 bay leaf
10 curry leaves
   (fresh are best,
   but dried will do)
1 green chilli,
   finely chopped
1 small onion,
   finely chopped
4 garlic cloves,
   finely chopped
30g ginger, peeled
   and finely grated
1 large plum tomato,
   roughly chopped
Fine sea salt
1 tbsp chopped
   coriander, to garnish
Rotis or chapatis,
   to serve

Tagliatelle with Mushrooms, Brandy & Green Peppercorns

If it is almost instant gratification you need, this dish is ideal: once the pasta is cooked and ready, it's really a matter of minutes before you have something immensely satisfying. If brandy isn't something you keep in stock, you could try whisky, but a dry white wine would also do the trick.

When it comes to the peppercorns, please try to stick to the recipe as best you can: green peppercorns are black peppercorns that haven't been through the drying and maturing process, but their flavour is more vegetal than warming. I use dried here, which are slightly weaker. If you can't find the green ones, 2 teaspoons of coarsely ground black pepper would be a reasonable alternative, but, please, never ever use pink peppercorns for this – unless you want a mouth so numb that you feel you've visited a backstreet dentist.

SERVES 2

250g dried tagliatelle

For the sauce
1 tbsp olive oil
30g unsalted butter
1 onion, very
    finely chopped
250g chestnut
    mushrooms,
    finely sliced
1 tbsp dried green
    peppercorns
100ml brandy
150ml chicken stock
150ml double cream
Fine sea salt and
    freshly ground
    black pepper

Cook the pasta according to the packet instructions, but make sure you do so in very salty water. Once the pasta is cooked, drain it, reserving 50ml or so of the cooking water, and have the pasta handy.

For the sauce, heat a medium frying pan over a high heat and, once it is hot, add the oil and butter, along with the onion, mushrooms and peppercorns. Cook, stirring and tossing the pan constantly, for a few minutes until the mushrooms wilt down and the onion is just slightly softened and coloured. Add the brandy and allow it to bubble and evaporate almost entirely – if it sets on fire that's fine: just watch your eyebrows. Add the chicken stock and allow that to bubble and almost entirely evaporate. Add the cream, allowing it to bubble for a minute, and then turn off the heat and season to taste. Add the pasta to the frying pan and stir to coat well – if the sauce is a little thick, let it down with the reserved pasta water. Serve immediately.

Mussels with Italian Salsiccia in Red Wine

There's something about the tactile eating of mussels that attaches you firmly to the earth and its produce: their light scent of the sea, the way the shell acts as both pick for pecking away at the tender meat and spoon for slurping up the cooking liquor. You might expect mussels in white wine or a curried sauce, but their flavour really stands up well to the depth of red wine, especially when lightly spiced with the fennel from the Italian salsiccia. Chervil is the lovechild of parsley and aniseed. It has a fairly mild flavour, which you might think wouldn't hold against the depth of red wine and sausage, but scattered over the finished dish it refreshes the flavour well. If you can't find chervil, use a mixture of dill and parsley.

Start by preparing the mussels. Scrape any lurking dirt from the shells and tug off any beards. Submerge the mussels in a bowl of lightly salted water. Any mussels that float must be discarded, along with any broken ones and any that stay open after they've been soaked for 10 minutes. Drain the mussels and set aside until required.

Remove and discard the skins from the sausages, and cut the sausages into small chunks. Have them handy.

Heat a large saucepan or casserole over a high heat and add the butter and oil. When the butter melts, add the shallots and fry, stirring frequently, for about 5 minutes or so – you want the shallots to colour lightly, but not catch. Don't worry that the butter might burn a little; it only serves to add more depth of flavour. Add the sausage chunks and go at them with a wooden spoon to break them down slightly, cooking them with the shallots for a few minutes, just until a little browned.

Add the wine and allow it to come to the boil, then reduce the heat to medium and throw in the mussels. Put the lid on and cook for just 3 or 4 minutes, until the mussels have opened. Scatter over the chervil and a generous pinch of salt. Serve immediately with the bread.

SERVES 4–6

1kg fresh mussels
4 salsiccia (fresh
 Italian sausage)
40g unsalted butter
1 tbsp olive oil
2 banana shallots,
 thinly sliced
250ml red wine
 (Pinot Noir
 or Chianti)
Small handful of
 fresh chervil,
 roughly chopped
Sea salt flakes
Crusty white bread,
 torn and buttered,
 to serve

Breakfast Ramen

Ramen takes different forms that vary from region to region of Japan, so I feel shameless in entirely hijacking the recipe to come up with something so westernised. I wanted to marry that idea of a wholesome bowlful of noodle soup with something I find equally as comforting: the English breakfast.

SERVES 2

For the broth

8 streaky bacon rashers,
  roughly chopped
1 tbsp sunflower oil
4 garlic cloves, halved
30g fresh ginger, peeled
  and finely grated
1 spring onion,
  finely sliced
1 tsp Chinese
  five-spice powder
2 tbsp dark soy sauce
3 tbsp light soy sauce
2 tbsp brown miso paste
2 tsp Worcestershire sauce
2 tsp toasted sesame oil
1 litre chicken stock
415g can baked beans

To serve

150g ramen noodles
2 large eggs
Small handful of spinach
1 carrot, peeled
  and chopped into
  fine batons
1 spring onion, chopped
  into fine batons
2.5cm piece of fresh
  ginger, chopped
  into fine batons

For the broth, heat a large saucepan over a medium heat and, once it is hot, add the bacon. Allow the pieces to cook until slightly crispy and the fat has seeped out of them. Add the oil to the pan, crank up the heat to high, add the garlic cloves, ginger, onion and five-spice powder and stir-fry for just a minute or two. Stir in the soy sauces, miso paste, Worcestershire sauce and sesame oil, then add the chicken stock and baked beans. Bring the soup to the boil, reduce the heat to low and cook for 45 minutes.

For the noodles, fill another saucepan with water and bring to the boil. Have two bowls of cold water ready. Boil the noodles for 3–5 minutes (double-check the packet instructions), then scoop out – I use kitchen tongs – and put into one of the bowls of cold water to prevent the noodles from becoming slimy. Allow the water in the pan to return to the boil, then add the eggs and boil for 7 minutes. Remove and add them to the second bowl of cold water to keep the yolks soft.

Divide the noodles between two bowls – I swirl them around onto kitchen tongs, then slide them, in a neat bundle, into the bowl. Add a small handful of spinach and spoon the hot soup over the top. Add the chopped carrot, onion and ginger, then peel and halve the eggs and add them to the bowls. Serve immediately.

Devil's Curry

This Malaysian curry is, as the title suggests, seriously spicy. Of course the chillies give it heat, but the spice is far deeper than just a startling burn. Thanks to the lemongrass, ginger, galangal and vinegar, this curry transcends. From the title, you'd also probably expect this to be a deep, demonic red, but the turmeric turns the sauce into a vibrant, sunny yellow – perhaps luring you into a false sense of security.

For the paste, remove and discard the woody ends of the lemongrass stalks and chop the rest roughly. Peel the ginger (I don't bother to peel the turmeric or galangal): the best way is to use the tip of a teaspoon to scrape off the skin. Put these and the remaining paste ingredients into a food processor and pulse to a smooth, pungent paste – you might need to scrape down the sides of the bowl once or twice to ensure everything is incorporated.

Heat a glug of oil in a large flameproof casserole over a high heat and, once the oil is hot, add the mustard seeds. Fry, stirring briefly and occasionally, until the seeds start to pop violently. Allow the seeds to continue frying noisily for a minute, then add the paste. Fry, stirring every minute or so, until the paste dries out – a good few minutes. Reduce the heat to medium, add the chicken pieces and stir to coat, and fry for a further 10 minutes. Stir in the sugar, add the potatoes and chicken stock – if the stock doesn't quite cover everything, add enough water to ensure the potatoes are just covered. Bring the curry to the boil, reduce to a simmer and cook, uncovered, for 30 minutes or until the potatoes are tender – give the pan a stir every once in a while.

Remove the pan from the heat and allow to sit for 15 minutes before serving with a scattering of fresh coriander.

SERVES 4

For the paste

3 lemongrass stalks

40g fresh ginger

30g fresh galangal

30g fresh turmeric

2 tbsp fish sauce

10–15 whole dried chillies

50ml cider vinegar

3 banana shallots, peeled

6 garlic cloves, peeled

1 tsp ground turmeric

2 tbsp sunflower oil

For the curry

Sunflower oil, for frying

1 tbsp yellow
  mustard seeds

1kg chicken thigh
  fillets, diced

2 tbsp dark brown sugar

500g new potatoes,
  quartered

500ml chicken stock

Small handful of
  coriander, to serve

Pan-fried Salmon with Lemongrass Sambal & Roasted Broccoli

Sambal is a condiment widely used in Indonesia, Malaysia and Sri Lanka. Each area has countless different versions, with different names depending on how it is prepared and the ingredients used. This version is a mixture of several recipes I've tried or tasted over the past few years, and it is damn good with fried fish.

SERVES 2

For the broccoli
300g tenderstem
   broccoli
1 lemongrass stalk
1 tbsp chilli or
   sunflower oil
2 tbsp light soy sauce

For the sambal
1 lemongrass stalk
30g fresh ginger,
   peeled
1 banana shallot,
   peeled and
   quartered
4 garlic cloves
4 red chillies
1 tsp Thai
   shrimp paste
1 tbsp light soy sauce
Juice and zest
   of 1 lime
60g runny honey
50ml white
   wine vinegar

For the salmon
2 large salmon
   fillets, skin on
2 tbsp sunflower oil
Sea salt flakes

Preheat the oven to 200°C/180°C fan/gas mark 6.

Place the broccoli on a baking tray. Bash the lemongrass and cut it in half, add it to the tray with the broccoli, and toss together with the oil and soy. Roast for 15–20 minutes, just until the broccoli has gone slightly crispy at the edges. Remove and discard the lemongrass.

For the sambal, bash the lemongrass stalk with the spine of a knife to help release the flavoursome oils. Chop the lemongrass in half, then slice each half lengthways to give 4 long quarters. Put the ginger, shallot, garlic, chillies and shrimp paste into a small food processor (or use a pestle and mortar) and blitz to a rough paste.

Heat a dry saucepan over a medium-high heat and add the paste mixture with the quartered lemongrass. Fry, stirring frequently, for a few minutes, until the paste starts to look dry and on the verge of colouring. Stir in the soy, lime juice and zest, honey and vinegar, and cook, stirring, for a minute or two. Remove from the heat.

Score shallow lines into the skin of the salmon fillets, a few millimetres apart, then season each fillet well with salt. Heat the oil in a frying pan over a medium heat, and once the oil is hot, add the salmon, skin-side down. Gently press the fillet against the base of the pan for 30 seconds to stop the skin curling and to help it crisp up, then leave to cook for a few minutes. When most of their deep coral pink colour has turned pale, flip the fillets over and fry for a further minute or so.

Reheat the sambal if necessary. Serve the salmon fillet with the sambal and the broccoli on the side.

Spiced Chicken in Milk

Chicken braised in milk is the best, most succulent chicken I have ever eaten. The milk not only creates steam in the pot, preventing the meat from drying out, but the slightly acidic nature of the milk also helps to tenderise the meat. The aim, believe it or not, is to curdle the milk to create a thick and flavoursome sauce. Because the spices are cooked slowly, they soften in flavour, so the sauce isn't bold like a curry; it's a haunting, gently warming sauce.

Preheat the oven to 190°C/170°C fan/gas mark 5.

Choose a lidded ovenproof pot that will just accommodate the whole chicken. Heat the oil in the pot over a high heat. Season the chicken with salt, then add it to the pot and fry on all sides until deeply browned – I use kitchen tongs to move the chicken about and hold it in place. You mustn't rush this part. Add the remaining ingredients, except the fresh coriander and lemon wedges, along with a generous pinch of salt and pepper, and bring to the boil. Pop on the lid and cook in the oven for 1½ hours.

To serve, simply sprinkle over some chopped fresh coriander – and perhaps a little lemon juice – then plonk the pot on the table and dig in. Alternatively, you can remove the chicken from the pot, shred all the meat off the bones, then return the meat to the sauce and serve.

SERVES 4

2 tbsp sunflower oil
1.5kg chicken
30g fresh ginger,
   finely chopped
1 onion, finely sliced
2 tsp ground coriander
2 tsp fennel seeds
2 tsp ground paprika
1 tsp ground turmeric
6 garlic cloves,
   whole but peeled
Small handful of
   dried curry leaves
125g cashew nuts
Zest of 1 large
   unwaxed lemon
600ml full-fat milk
Fine sea salt and coarsely
   ground black pepper

To serve
Chopped coriander leaves
Lemon wedges for
   squeezing (optional)

Chicken, Apricot &
Scotch Bonnet Jollof

Jollof is a West African rice dish, not too dissimilar to jambalaya. This isn't an authentic version, but the inspiration is true. Scotch Bonnet chillies can be ferociously hot, so do go steady with them. I like it very hot, especially bearing in mind the sweetness from those apricots, which helps to balance it all out.

SERVES 6

500g chicken thigh
   fillets, diced
1 tbsp sunflower oil
1 onion, roughly chopped
3 garlic cloves, sliced
1–2 Scotch Bonnet chillies
2 tsp ground ginger
2 tsp ground cumin
1 tsp ground cinnamon
1 tbsp dried thyme
2 tsp ground coriander
1 tsp ground turmeric
1 tbsp tomato purée
250g tomatoes,
   roughly chopped
350g basmati rice
700ml chicken stock
150g soft dried apricots,
   roughly chopped
100g okra
Fine sea salt and freshly
   ground black pepper

green pepper salsa
1 green pepper, seeds
   removed, finely diced
1 spring onion,
   finely sliced
Juice of 1 lime
15g coriander,
   roughly chopped
Sea salt flakes

Preheat the oven to 200°C/180°C fan/gas mark 6.

Season the chicken thigh chunks generously with salt and pepper. Heat the oil in a large heavy-based casserole or ovenproof saucepan. Fry the chicken in the hot oil until golden on all sides. Remove the chicken from the pan and set aside until needed.

Keep the same pan over a low heat, add the onion and cook until soft – about 8 minutes. Add the garlic, chillies and spices, and cook for a minute or so, until fragrant. Add the tomato purée and cook, stirring, for a further minute, then add the chopped tomatoes and cook for 2 minutes before adding the rice. Stir the rice well, ensuring the grains are completely coated in all the spicy juices. Add the stock and apricots, mixing well, and then bring the pan to the boil. Once the liquid is boiling, remove the pan from the heat and return the chicken to the pan. Cover with a lid, or foil, and cook in the oven for 40 minutes.

To make the salsa, mix all the ingredients together and season to taste.

When the rice is cooked, remove the pan from the oven and add the okra. Cover again and return to the oven for a further 5 minutes.

Serve immediately from the pan with the zingy salsa spooned over the top.

Duck Breast with Pomegranate & Basil Tabbouleh

Duck breast is so easy to cook, but often people are a little wary of it. I suppose that fear isn't ill-founded; there's nothing worse than tough, overcooked duck breast, but with this method it's almost impossible to ruin. The key is to put the duck into a cold, dry pan, skin-side down and render the fat slowly over a low heat. The tabbouleh is beautifully sharp and balances the rich meat well.

SERVES 2

2 duck breasts
Fine sea salt

For the tabbouleh
45g bulgar wheat
300g plum tomatoes
4 spring onions
Juice of 1 lemon
½ tsp ground
   black pepper
½ tsp ground allspice
½ tsp ground
   cinnamon
¼ tsp freshly
   grated nutmeg
Pinch of ground cloves
100g flat-leaf
   parsley leaves,
   finely chopped
40g basil leaves,
   finely chopped
75ml extra virgin
   olive oil
Seeds from
   ½ pomegranate

Rinse the bulgar wheat under the cold tap until the water runs clear, then put into a bowl and cover by 1cm with boiling water. Cover with clingfilm and leave to soak for 20 minutes.

Score a very fine crisscross pattern into the duck fat and season with salt. Place the duck, skin-side down, into a cold frying pan, then set it over a low heat. Fry the duck for 20–25 minutes, without turning, until the fat seeps out and the skin becomes very crispy and golden – drain the fat away twice during cooking (keep it for next time you roast potatoes). Flip over the duck breasts, crank up the heat to medium-high, and fry for a further 2–3 minutes. Transfer the duck to a plate and leave to rest, uncovered, for 5 minutes.

Meanwhile, roughly chop the tomatoes and finely slice the spring onions. Put all but a few spring onion slices and all the tomatoes into a bowl. Add the lemon juice, spices, most of the parsley, the basil, olive oil and pomegranate seeds.

Use a fork to fluff up the bulgar wheat and add it to the bowl. Toss everything together, season well and set aside until needed.

Slice the rested duck breast and serve with a mound of tabbouleh. Finish with a scattering of the reserved chopped parsley and spring onion.

Indian Shepherd's Pie with a Sag Aloo Top

The only worry with a book on comfort food is that most families already have their own recipes for the favourites. How can I offer something reassuring and familiar, but with enough of a twist to entice you to make it? Shepherd's pie is one of those recipes, but rather than give you the regular version we know and love, I'm making it with spice. This is something else.

Heat a large sauté pan or shallow casserole over a high heat and, once it is hot, add the butter, cloves, cumin seeds, cinnamon stick, bay leaves and peppercorns. Fry, stirring frequently, until the bay leaves start to crackle and there is a strong spice aroma. Add the onions and carrot and continue to fry, tossing the pan every so often, for 5 minutes, just until the vegetables are hot – there's really no need to cook them until they soften, provided you chopped them finely enough.

Mix in the ginger, garlic and tomato purée and fry for a further minute, just until the garlic smells strongly. Pour in the stock, bring to the boil and cook until the liquid has reduced by a third. Add the remaining ingredients and 1 teaspoon salt and put into a roasting dish. Don't bother to wash the pan out – use it for the topping.

Preheat the oven to 200°C/180°C fan/gas mark 6.

For the sag aloo top, put the potatoes into a large saucepan, cover them with cold water and add a generous pinch of salt. Bring to the boil, boil for 10 minutes, then drain. Put the oil and butter into the sauté pan and set over a high heat. Once the butter melts, add the spices and fry until the mustard seeds start to pop. Add the potatoes and water – the water will sizzle and evaporate quickly. Stir the potatoes in the spiced liquid, then add the spinach; turn off the heat and allow the spinach to wilt in the residual heat for a few minutes.

Pile the sag aloo on top of the lamb and lentil filling. Bake for 30–40 minutes, until the filling is bubbling. If the potatoes start to burn before the filling is ready, cover the dish with foil.

SERVES 4–6

50g unsalted butter

4 cloves

2½ tsp cumin seeds

½ cinnamon stick

2 dried bay leaves

4 black peppercorns

2 onions,
  very finely chopped

1 carrot,
  very finely chopped

40g fresh ginger,
  finely grated

4 garlic cloves, minced

1 tbsp tomato purée

1 litre chicken stock

1 tbsp garam masala

2 x 250g sachets
  cooked Puy lentils

250g minced lamb

250g frozen garden
  peas, defrosted

Fine sea salt

For the sag aloo top

1kg red-skin potatoes,
  cut into 2.5cm cubes

1 tbsp sunflower oil

50g unsalted butter

1 tsp cumin seeds

1 tsp ground turmeric

1 tsp black mustard seeds

200ml water

200g baby leaf spinach

something spicy

Minced Beef & Horseradish Pie

I'm a Lancashire lad, so for me the pie is almost an auspicious symbol. Much as I appreciate a range of fillings, I personally believe that it'd be hard to find a pie to compete with a simple minced beef with its silky gravy and short, crisp pastry. I add the horseradish sauce here because I like the heat and slight sourness, but if you prefer to leave it out, feel free to do so. And when it comes to a sauce on the side – I know this is a controversial subject – it has to be a tangy brown sauce for me.

SERVES 4–6

For the pastry
250g cold unsalted
    butter, cubed
500g plain flour
1 large egg
2 tbsp horseradish sauce
3 tbsp cold water

For the filling
40g unsalted butter
2 onions,
    roughly chopped
2 tbsp plain flour
700ml beef stock
1 tbsp Worcestershire
    sauce
1 tbsp horseradish sauce
500g minced beef
Fine sea salt and
    coarsely ground
    black pepper
1 small egg, beaten,
    to glaze

For the pastry, rub the butter into the flour with 1 teaspoon salt until it resembles breadcrumbs. Make a well in the centre. Beat together the egg, horseradish sauce and water and add to the dry ingredients. Use a dough scraper or knife to cut the wet ingredients into the dry. If it doesn't quite come together, add a little more water. Once the dough comes together roughly, gently work for a few seconds until smooth. Flatten into a disc, wrap in clingfilm and chill for an hour.

For the filling, first make the gravy. Heat the butter in a saucepan over a medium heat and, once it melts, add the onions. Cook, stirring occasionally, until the onions are very soft but mostly uncoloured – about 20 minutes. Increase the heat to high and add the flour to the onions, stirring to mix well. Add the stock, bring to the boil, then reduce to a gentle simmer and cook until the liquid has reduced by half. Remove from the heat, add the Worcestershire and horseradish sauces and season to taste – remember to make it ever so slightly salty so that the beef doesn't dilute it too much. Stir in the beef to mix well, then remove from the heat and allow it to cool.

Preheat the oven to 200°C/180°C fan/gas mark 6.

Roll out half of the pastry on a floured worktop until reasonably thin – don't be too eager, but don't make it too thick. Line a 23cm pie tin with the rolled-out pastry, allowing the excess to hang over the sides. Pile the filling into the pie dish, then roll out the remaining pastry and use it to cover the filling. Remove the surplus pastry and crimp the edges. Glaze the pie with the beaten egg, then cut a cross or hole into the top to allow steam to escape. Bake the pie for 35–40 minutes, or until the pastry is golden brown and the filling is very hot (I push a knife into the centre of the pie, and if the blade feels too hot to touch, the pie is ready).

something crunchy

Crumbs

Crumbs remind me of a particular dinner lady at primary school. She was a handsome woman, a typical Lancashire lass of the 1990s, whose huge heart wasn't at all mirrored by her stern face. She knew my parents, so always gave me what I imagined to be a wink – though I never could tell whether it was affection or a physical tick.

Now, you can imagine the crumbs in a primary school dinner hall. It was as though we kids, red-cheeked and exhausted by the over-zealous teachers, managed to produce more crumbs in weight than the food from which they fell. It was that same dinner lady who would pilfer all the scraps for her chickens. She'd wipe away the traces of our frenzied lunch, raking the crumbs into the pocket of her pinny. We'd look on, hands frozen halfway between plate and mouth, flabbergasted by the crazy lady.

Whenever there were leftovers from the school canteen, she would do the rounds, bellowing, 'Who wants another potato croquette?' A furious sea of polyester cuffs would thrash about the hall. The croquette-to-ratbag ratio was vastly uneven, yet somehow I always ended up in possession of an extra golden nugget.

Those potato croquettes saw the beginning of my obsession with crunchy food. It's an obsession that hasn't ever left me, not that I'd want it to; and it was only amplified by my parents owning a fish and chip shop, where I'd be so grateful for the warmth of a battered fish, its crust thick and crunchy, its flesh so tender and flaking.

Whether it's the simple tearing of a fresh white baguette with its snowfall of crumbs onto your jumper, or the sophisticated well-seasoned crust of a Milanese chop, crunchy food is so satisfying. It feels a bit naughty, too; it isn't necessarily the healthiest food to enjoy, but that's partly what is so gratifying about it. If you're going to sin, you may as well do it properly.

Cumin, Fennel & Nigella Seed Onion Rings with Pomegranate Molasses Chutney

Much as I love an onion ring, after you've eaten a few they can start to taste a little bland. That is certainly not a concern with this recipe: with every bite a different seed pops in your mouth, releasing its flavour. And if that weren't enough, the chutney packs quite a punch. That's why I use red onions here; they're a little sweeter and complement the spices so well.

SERVES 4

2 large red onions
Sunflower oil, for frying

For the batter
125g self-raising flour
2 tsp baking powder
125ml milk
125ml water
1 tsp sea salt flakes
½ tsp ground turmeric
1 tsp fennel seeds
1 tbsp nigella seeds
1 tbsp cumin seeds

For the chutney
300ml water
75g pomegranate
  molasses
50g dark
  muscovado sugar
½ tsp sea salt flakes
½ tsp chilli powder
½ tsp ground cumin
½ tsp ground ginger

Slice the onions into 1cm-thick discs and separate the individual rings. Place the rings into a bowl of cold water.

For the batter, sift together the flour and baking powder into a mixing bowl. In a separate jug, mix the water and milk together, then slowly pour the liquid into the flour, whisking constantly. It's best to add a little of the liquid first, mix the batter to a very thick paste, then slowly slacken it to the consistency of thick double cream. Add the salt and spices and set aside to rest while you prepare the chutney.

Put all the ingredients for the chutney into a small saucepan and bring to the boil, stirring. Reduce the heat to a brisk simmer and allow the chutney to reduce until it is of a thin syrup consistency – it should take about 15 minutes. Set aside to cool.

Heat a deep-fat fryer to 180°C, or pour about 4cm of the sunflower oil into a wok and use a food thermometer. When the oil is hot, dredge the onion rings through the batter, coating them well, and drop them into the hot oil. Fry the onion rings, a few at a time, until deeply golden – this takes no time at all – then remove with a slotted spoon and transfer to a plate lined with kitchen paper to blot off any excess oil. Serve immediately with the chutney.

Leftover Batter

At the end of a shift in our chippy, local village lads on their bikes would cycle up to the window and ask for any scraps (bits of batter from the fryers). They'd absolutely drench them with salt and vinegar, and ride off contented. There will be some batter left at the end of this recipe, but don't waste it: drizzle it into the fryer, frying it until deeply golden, then drain and serve with the remaining chutney, or plenty of lemon juice and salt.

Chicken Miso Milanese
with Soba Noodles

Chicken Milanese – which I prefer over veal – is one of the best inventions in the realm of comfort food: a flattened slab of meat (an escalope) coated in breadcrumbs, then fried. When done perfectly, the outside should be an orange gold with almost impossible crispness while the inside is tender beyond belief and perfectly seasoned. The problem with it is, however, inconsistency. I'm saddened to admit that I've had more bad Milanese than good, but this version makes your mind fizz. Not only is the gentle cooking heat guaranteed to give a crisp finish, but also the miso paste will ensure the meat sings with flavour – so much so that I don't add any extra salt at all to the meat.

Put the chicken between two pieces of baking paper and hammer flat with a rolling pin – you want it to be 1–1.5cm thick all over.

Put the miso paste, egg white and soy sauce into a mixing bowl and stir well to combine. Add the chicken to the bowl and turn it to coat evenly and completely with the miso paste. Leave to marinate while you cook the noodles.

Bring a medium saucepan of water to the boil and add the noodles. Cook the noodles for 3–5 minutes (though do check the packet instructions), then strain and tip into a bowl of cold water. Set aside until needed. Combine all of the other ingredients for the noodles in a small bowl and set aside.

Put the breadcrumbs and 1 teaspoon salt onto a plate and turn the chicken in the breadcrumbs until well coated, then dip the chicken back into the miso mixture, then into the breadcrumbs a second time.

Heat a frying pan over a medium heat and add the butter with the oil. As soon as the butter melts, add the chicken to the pan and fry for 4–5 minutes each side, or until deeply golden brown. Remove the chicken from the pan and place on a piece of kitchen paper to blot off any excess oil.

Wipe out the frying pan and place it back over a high heat. Add the noodle sauce mixture and fry for just a minute until fragrant, then throw in the drained noodles and beansprouts with a splash of water and toss until evenly coated and heated through. Serve with the chicken Milanese.

SERVES 1

For the chicken Milanese
1 chicken breast
3 tbsp brown rice
   miso paste
1 egg white
2 tsp light soy sauce
40g panko
   breadcrumbs,
   finely crushed
50g unsalted butter
1 tbsp sunflower oil
Fine sea salt

For the noodles
100g buckwheat
   soba noodles
1 garlic clove, minced
30g fresh ginger,
   finely grated
1 bird's eye chilli,
   left whole
1 tbsp brown rice
   miso paste
1 tbsp dark soy sauce
1 tsp light soy sauce
1 tsp sesame oil
50g beansprouts

Butterbeans in Romesco Sauce on Toast with Honey

The first time I ate Romesco sauce was with grilled hake and aubergine fritters, finished with some honey. It was cooked for me by José Pizarro, when he was a guest chef on a TV show I was presenting. Out of all the things I've had cooked for me in the rushed, hectic television environment (where, often, the food doesn't taste as good as it should) it was the most delicious. In fact, it's up there with the most incredible things I've ever eaten. Whenever I make Romesco sauce now, I always think of the wonderful José and his love of good food.

As a dish, this takes a little effort and preferably a good food processor, but it's all worth it when you find yourself chowing down on the most delicious version of beans on toast imaginable. I top mine with some finely grated Manchego cheese and a drizzle of golden honey.

SERVES 2

400g can cooked
  butterbeans, rinsed
  and drained
Small handful of
  flat-leaf parsley,
  finely chopped
2 thick slices of
  sourdough, toasted

For the Romesco sauce
40g blanched almonds
1 tbsp olive oil
40g stale bread, torn
  into bite-sized pieces
2 garlic cloves, sliced
250g roasted red
  peppers (from a jar,
  drained weight)
½ tsp smoked paprika
1 tbsp sherry vinegar
100ml extra virgin
  olive oil
Fine sea salt and freshly
  ground black pepper ▶

For the sauce, heat a small dry frying pan over a high heat and add the almonds. Toast the almonds, tossing the pan frequently, until lightly browned. Tip them into a food processor.

Heat the tablespoon of olive oil in the same frying pan over a medium-high heat, add the bread and toast for 2 minutes or until the bread is beginning to turn a golden brown. Add the garlic, stir well and cook for 30 seconds – just until the garlic smells strongly. Remove the pan from the heat.

Add the bread and garlic to the food processor along with the red peppers, smoked paprika, sherry vinegar and extra virgin olive oil. Add a good pinch of salt and some pepper. Blend until smooth.

Put the drained butterbeans into a saucepan. Add the Romesco sauce with a splash of water and warm over a gentle heat, stirring all the time. Don't have the heat too high or the sauce may split.

When the sauce is warm, remove it from the heat and stir through the parsley. Put the toasted sourdough on a serving plate and divide the butter beans in Romesco sauce between the slices.

Serve topped with
the grated cheese,
drizzled with honey
and sprinkled with a
little smoked paprika
and salt flakes.

To serve
30g Manchego,
 finely grated
Runny honey,
 to drizzle (I like
 orange blossom here)
Smoked paprika
Sea salt flakes

BLT Italian Style

The BLT is a personal favourite of mine – one which, as a child, I used to pray to find, along with peanut butter and jelly, in my lunchbox. This is a more sophisticated version of that classic. Radicchio, in place of regular lettuce, adds its slightly bitter tang, which marries well with the boldness of the olives, capers and sundried tomatoes.

For the mayo, mix the olives, capers, mayo and parsley in a bowl. Set aside until needed.

Heat a large frying pan over a medium heat. Once the pan is hot, add the pancetta or bacon rashers and fry until coloured, flipping once – I do this in two batches so as not to overcrowd the pan. Put the cooked rashers on a plate lined with a sheet of kitchen paper to blot dry. Don't remove the fat from the pan, and leave the pan on the heat.

Slice the ciabatta rolls fully open and fry in the bacon fat, cut-side down, for a minute or two, just until slightly golden.

To assemble, spread the mayo on both halves of the ciabatta. On the bottom half of ciabatta place the sundried tomatoes, then the pancetta, then the radicchio. Drizzle with a little balsamic vinegar to sweeten, then top with the second half of ciabatta and cut in half to serve.

SERVES 2

For the mayo

50g pitted black olives, finely chopped

2 tbsp non-pareil capers, roughly chopped

3 heaped tbsp mayo

1 tbsp finely chopped flat-leaf parsley

For the sandwich

8 smoked pancetta (or streaky bacon) rashers

2 ciabatta rolls

50g sundried tomatoes (drained weight), roughly chopped

4 radicchio leaves

Drizzle of balsamic vinegar

something crunchy

Korean Disco Fries

Chips and gravy may feel like a British tradition, but it's even more popular across the pond. In Canada, poutine is a staple snack of chips, thick gravy and cheese curds. In New Jersey they serve 'ghetto poutine' or disco fries, made with a mozzarella cheese sauce rather than the curds. My version, with a Korean gochujang-spiked gravy and fermented cabbage (kimchi), is comfort with a punch.

The name disco fries, incidentally, comes from stumbling into a takeaway after a night of heavy boozing, in inebriated pursuit of carbs, something I wouldn't know anything about…

A note on the chips: I poach mine in hot oil before frying them until golden. This makes the insides unbelievably fluffy, and the outsides golden and crisp. If you're not a fan of making your own chips, I wouldn't complain if you were to use oven chips; while my twice-cooked chips are hard to beat, the gravy is what this dish is all about.

SERVES 2

For the gravy
50g unsalted butter
1 banana shallot,
  finely chopped
1 garlic clove, minced
2 tbsp plain flour
2 tbsp tomato ketchup
2 tbsp gochujang
  (Korean chilli paste)
1 tbsp cider vinegar
1 tsp Worcestershire
  sauce
1 tbsp dark soy sauce
500g chicken stock
500g beef stock

For the cheese sauce
200ml evaporated milk
50g Monterey Jack or
  medium Cheddar
50g Stilton
Fine sea salt and freshly
  ground black pepper ▶

For the gravy, heat the butter in a medium saucepan over a medium-high heat. Once the butter has melted, add the shallot and fry for about 3 minutes, or until softened. Add the garlic and flour and stir to mix, then add the ketchup, gochujang, vinegar, Worcestershire sauce and soy sauce and stir until thick. Stir in the chicken stock, then the beef stock. Bring the gravy to the boil, then reduce to a rapid simmer and cook for 20–30 minutes, until the gravy is thick and has reduced by two-thirds. Test the seasoning, though this really shouldn't need any more salt. Set aside and keep warm until needed.

For the cheese sauce, bring the evaporated milk to the boil in a small saucepan. Once it is boiling, reduce the heat to medium-low and add the cheese. Stir the sauce until the cheese has melted completely. Season to taste, then set aside and keep warm until needed.

Heat the oil in the deep-fat fryer to 110°C. Peel the potatoes and cut them into chips 1cm thick. When the deep-fat fryer is up to temperature, add the potatoes and fry for 15 minutes. Remove the chips (I just lift out the frying basket and hook it onto the side, out of the oil) and increase the heat to 180°C. Return the chips to the fryer, and fry for a further 5–10 minutes, or until golden brown and crispy. Transfer to a plate lined with kitchen paper to blot off any excess oil.

To assemble, layer the chips, gravy, kimchi and sweetcorn (no need to heat those) in a large bowl, and top with the cheese sauce and coriander. Eat immediately.

For the twice-cooked chips
1kg (about 6)
  Maris Piper potatoes
Sunflower oil, for deep-frying

To assemble
200g kimchi (if you can't find
  kimchi, use sauerkraut)
½ can (198g) sweetcorn,
  drained
Small handful of coriander
  leaves, roughly chopped

something crunchy

Lazy Man's Bibimbap

Bibimbap, literally meaning 'mixed rice', is a classic Korean comfort-food dish of rice, mixed vegetables and meat. Delicious as all that sounds, it isn't as basic as you may think: the rice is fried until crispy, adding an extra layer of texture. Ordinarily, the vegetables are cooked individually, but I've tried to make it easier by chucking them into the pan all at once. And, to take it a step closer towards doing absolutely nothing, I use packets of ready-cooked rice.

Preheat the oven to 160°C/140°C fan/gas mark 3.

For the sauce, simply combine the ingredients in a small bowl and have handy.

Slice the steak and place in another bowl. Coat with 1 tablespoon of the sauce, the extra tablespoon of soy sauce and the salt and leave to marinate while you cook the vegetables.

Heat a large ovenproof frying pan over a high heat and, once it is hot, add 1 tablespoon of the sesame oil and the mushrooms, peas and beansprouts – but keep them separate, don't mix them up. Reduce the heat to medium and cook, stirring occasionally, until the mushrooms are soft and the peas slightly charred. Transfer the vegetables to a plate, still keeping them separate. Put into the oven to keep warm.

Wipe out the pan and return it to a high heat. When the pan is very hot, add the steak and stir-fry just until the meat is seared. Transfer to a plate and put into the warm oven.

Return the pan to a medium heat, add another tablespoon of the sesame oil and the rice. Level the rice out and cook for 15 minutes, without disturbing, until the rice in contact with the pan is crispy. Remove from the heat and arrange the vegetables and steak at four separate points on top of the rice, leaving a little bit of bare rice for the egg. Put the pan into the oven to keep warm.

Heat the remaining sesame oil in a smaller frying pan over a medium-high heat. Once the oil is hot, break in the egg and allow the white to set – spooning a little of the hot oil over the yolk helps to cook the white on top. As soon as the white is completely cooked through but the yolk still runny, lift the egg and place it on top of the rice in the large pan with everything else. Drizzle over the sauce and serve.

SERVES 2

1 sirloin steak,
  fat removed
1 tbsp light soy sauce
½ tsp fine sea salt
3 tbsp toasted
  sesame oil
150g shiitake
  mushrooms,
  finely sliced
150g sugar snap peas
150g beansprouts
500g ready-cooked
  basmati rice
1 large egg

For the sauce
1 tbsp gochujang
  (Korean chilli paste)
1 tbsp sesame oil
1 tbsp light soy sauce
1 tbsp runny honey
1 garlic clove, minced
30g fresh ginger,
  finely grated
1 tbsp black
  sesame seeds

something crunchy

Fish Finger Tacos with Watermelon Salsa & Avocado Cream

I know the ingredients list is long here, but this is really worth that little bit of effort. The result is the crunchiest, most decadent tacos I've ever had. If you want to speed this up a little, you could use frozen fish fingers, but they'll not be anywhere near as good as these.

SERVES 6

For the avocado cream

2 ripe avocados,
  peeled and stoned
150ml soured cream
2 limes: juice of 2
  and zest of 1
1 garlic clove
Fine sea salt

For the fish fingers

400g hake fillet (or
  any firm white fish)
100g plain flour
1 tsp cayenne pepper
1 tsp ground cumin
1 tsp garlic salt
4 large eggs
300g panko
  breadcrumbs,
  crushed until
  a little finer
500ml sunflower
  oil, for frying ▶

Start by making the avocado cream. Put all the ingredients into a food processor and blitz until very smooth. Decant into a bowl, season to taste, and keep covered in the fridge until ready to use.

For the fish fingers, slice the fillet into 5cm-long, 2cm-wide strips. Prepare the coating ingredients. Mix the flour with the spices and garlic salt and put onto a plate or use a shallow dish. Beat the eggs in a shallow bowl. Put the breadcrumbs into another shallow bowl. Now the fun begins. Dip each strip of fish first into the flour, then into the egg and finally into the breadcrumbs. Once it is evenly coated in the breadcrumbs, dip the strip back into the egg, coat well and then dip again into the breadcrumbs to double-coat – it's a little bit more effort but so worth it for the crunchiest coating on your fish.

Make your salsa last, just before frying your fish. It tastes much better as fresh as possible. Mix all the ingredients together and season to taste. Get your serving ingredients ready at the same time.

Heat the oil in a large frying pan: there should be about 2.5cm of oil in the pan. Once the oil is shimmering gently, fry the fish fingers, in batches, until golden and crisp, about 1–2 minutes each side. Transfer to an oven tray and keep warm in a low oven while you fry the rest.

Heat the tortillas in a microwave or the oven until warm but soft and pliable.

Put all the individual components on the table and allow everyone to dig in and make their own tacos, filling warmed tortillas – do keep a watchful eye on the greedier members of your party and slap their hands away if they're overloading their plates.

For the watermelon salsa

1 red onion,
   very finely chopped

500g watermelon,
   cut into 1cm dice

1 green jalapeño chilli,
   finely chopped

Juice of 2 limes

15g coriander,
   roughly chopped

To serve

12 small tortillas

100g radishes, sliced

Jalapeño chillies
   (from a jar)

Small handful of
   coriander leaves,
   chopped

2 limes, cut
   into wedges

something crunchy

Korean BBQ Popcorn Chicken

Whether it's karaage in Japan or deep-fried wings in America's Deep South, it seems that many cultures proudly have some form of fried chicken dish. I've sampled so many, but this is my favourite.

I think the secret to any fried chicken is garlic salt, without which nothing seems quite right. As important is the batter – this version uses vodka and crushed crackers which ensure a crispiness that is almost beyond belief. A deep-fat fryer is a must for this recipe.

First make the BBQ sauce. Heat a saucepan over a medium-high heat and add the butter. As soon as it melts, add the shallots and fry, stirring occasionally, until softened but uncoloured. Add the garlic, sugar and vinegar and stir until well mixed, then add the remaining sauce ingredients and stir to combine. Bring to the boil, then remove from the heat and set aside until needed.

For the batter, put the cornflour, flour and cracker crumbs into a mixing bowl along with the garlic salt and toss to combine well. Mix the water and vodka in a jug, then slowly pour the liquid into the dry ingredients while whisking constantly – it's easier to get any lumps out while the batter is still a thick paste. Don't add all of the liquid in one go – you want this to be a fairly loose batter, but not extremely watery.

Heat the oil in a deep-fat fryer to 180°C.

For the chicken, put the cornflour and garlic salt onto a large plate or shallow dish and toss together. Toss the cubed chicken in the cornflour, then dip some of the pieces in batter. Fry for a few minutes until golden brown and very crispy – work in batches to avoid overcrowding the fryer. Transfer the fried chicken to a plate lined with kitchen paper to blot off the excess oil and keep warm while you cook the rest.

If the BBQ sauce has gone cold, quickly reheat it, and serve in a bowl with the fried chicken pieces piled around it. Finish by scattering over the spring onion slices and sesame seeds, if using.

SERVES 4

For the BBQ sauce
40g unsalted butter
2 banana shallots,
  finely chopped
2 garlic cloves, minced
3 tbsp dark brown sugar
2 tbsp cider vinegar
3 tbsp gochujang
  (Korean chilli paste)
100g tomato ketchup
50ml apple juice
1 tbsp light soy sauce
1 tbsp Worcestershire
  sauce

For the batter
80g cornflour
40g self-raising flour
40g Jacob's Cream
  Crackers, bashed
  to fine crumbs
1½ tsp garlic salt
220ml sparkling water
50ml vodka

For the chicken
Sunflower oil,
  for deep-frying
75g cornflour
½ tsp garlic salt
1kg chicken breasts,
  cut into 2cm cubes

To serve
2 spring onions,
  finely sliced
2 tbsp white sesame
  seeds (optional)

Chicken Curry Crispy Pancakes

I suppose this recipe is incriminating for my mother: now you all know that she must have given me crispy pancakes when I was small. Friends have reassured me that this wasn't child cruelty, and that they still crave that shop-bought pleasure from time to time. And, in her defence, these, like sweets, were a treat. If you too ever ate crispy pancakes as a child, this recipe is for you. Assembling the pancakes is a little fiddly, I admit, but it's completely worthwhile.

MAKES 4

For the curry

Olive or sunflower
  oil, for frying
1 large onion,
  finely chopped
200g chestnut
  mushrooms,
  finely sliced
2 tsp fenugreek seeds
2 garlic cloves, minced
2 tsp ground cumin
2 tsp ground coriander
1 tsp ground turmeric
1 tbsp mango chutney,
  plus extra to serve
1 tbsp tomato purée
6 chicken thigh fillets,
  cut into 1cm dice
1 red pepper,
  deseeded and diced
100ml double cream
100ml water
Sea salt flakes and
  coarsely ground
  black pepper

For the pancakes

100g plain flour
2 large eggs
300ml milk
1 egg, beaten, to
  seal the pancakes ▶

First make the curry filling. Heat 2 tablespoons oil in a saucepan over a high heat. Once the oil is hot, add the onion, mushrooms, fenugreek seeds and 1 teaspoon salt, then reduce the heat to medium-low. Cook, stirring occasionally, for 25–30 minutes, or until the onion is very soft and mushy.

Add the garlic, cumin, coriander and turmeric and stir-fry for a minute. Add the chutney and tomato purée, stirring well, and cook for a further minute. Add the chicken and red pepper and mix well, then pour in the cream and water. Bring to the boil, reduce to a simmer and cook down for 15 minutes. Season to taste, remove from the heat and allow to cool slightly.

Meanwhile, make the pancake batter. Put the flour into a mixing bowl and make a well in the centre. Add the 2 eggs and about 50ml of the milk and whisk to a smooth paste. Whisking constantly, slowly pour in the remaining milk to form a very smooth, loose batter.

Heat a medium frying pan over a medium-high heat and add a glug of oil. When the pan is hot, add a quarter of the batter and tilt the pan to spread the batter evenly over the base. Fry until the underside is lightly browned and little pinprick bubbles form on the surface. Do not flip the pancake: the top side needs to remain raw to ensure it sticks together when you add the filling. Carefully slide the pancake onto the worktop. Repeat with the remaining batter. Do not stack these pancakes up, otherwise they will stick together.

Preheat the oven to 200°C/180°C fan/gas mark 6 and line two baking sheets with baking paper.

To assemble, prepare a little production line: put the flour and salt, beaten egg and breadcrumbs for the coating on three separate plates. Take a pancake, raw-side up, and pile a quarter of the curry into the centre of it. Glaze the edges with the beaten egg and fold the pancake over the

filling to form a semi-circle, pressing the edges together tightly to seal – don't worry if the pancake doesn't seal entirely, but try to avoid too many holes in the seal. Repeat with the remaining pancakes and filling and then dip each pancake first into the flour, then into the egg, and finally into the breadcrumbs to coat completely. Transfer to the lined baking sheets.

Bake the pancakes for 40 minutes, until golden brown and puffed up. Serve immediately.

For the coating

100g plain flour mixed
  with ½ tsp fine sea salt
1 large egg, beaten
180g fine breadcrumbs

something crunchy

Scandi Salmon Pizza

Comfort food doesn't necessarily need to be stodgy or heavy (though I'd never complain about that). This is, in relative terms, a fairly wholesome, well-balanced pizza with a curiously refreshing flavour. The idea of Scandinavian food, for me, conjures images of lighter flavour combinations – that's what this is all about.

For the dough, put all the ingredients in a mixing bowl and bring together, either with a wooden spoon or your hands, into a scraggy mass – you can also do this in a mixer fitted with dough hook. Once the dough starts to come together, knead until very soft and elastic. Put the dough into a greased bowl, cover with clingfilm and leave to rise until doubled in size.

Meanwhile combine all the ingredients for the topping, except the salmon, until well mixed.

For the pickled cucumber, stir together the lemon juice, vinegar and sugar in a small bowl and add the fennel seeds, capers and cucumber slices. Mix well and leave to infuse.

Preheat the oven to 250°C/230°C fan/gas mark 9 and place a baking sheet or pizza stone into the oven to get hot.

Once the dough has doubled in size, dust a second baking sheet liberally with flour and roll out the dough to a disc about 23cm in diameter. Check the disc of dough isn't stuck down to the baking sheet – give the sheet a quick jerk back and forward to ensure the disc moves freely on the flour. Spread the cream cheese mixture over the dough and scatter over the diced salmon. Slide the pizza off the cold baking sheet and onto the hot baking sheet in the oven. Bake for 7–10 minutes until both base and salmon are cooked through. Scatter over the pickled cucumber just before serving.

SERVES 1–2

For the dough
120g strong white
    bread flour, plus
    extra for dusting
30g spelt flour
5g fast-action yeast
3g fine sea salt
90ml warm water

For the topping
150g full-fat
    cream cheese
3 anchovies from a can
    or jar, roughly chopped
1 tbsp chopped
    fresh dill fronds,
    plus extra to serve
1 tbsp chopped chives
Zest of ½ unwaxed lemon
1 tsp coarse black pepper
140g skinless salmon
    fillets, diced

For the pickled cucumber
Juice of 1 lemon
1 tbsp cider vinegar
1 tbsp caster sugar
1 tsp fennel seeds
1 tbsp non-pareil capers
½ cucumber, very thinly
    sliced in rounds

Chorizo, Jalapeño & Black Bean Croquettes

I suppose the title here is all wrong. Being flavoured with the piquant nip of chorizo and Manchego, I'm guessing they should take their Spanish name: croquetas. But I can't part with the school-dinner version. I remember the yelps of joy as we entered the dinner hall to see 'potato croquettes' scribbled hurriedly onto the blackboard; the bright orange cylinders of spud were adored by all. In my heart these will always be croquettes.

MAKES ABOUT 20

For the croquettes
30g unsalted butter
35g plain flour
350ml whole milk
1 tbsp tomato purée
2 tsp Dijon mustard
200g Manchego,
  coarsely grated
50ml double cream
200g chorizo picante,
  very finely chopped
100g (drained weight)
  black beans from a can
75g (drained weight)
  jalapeños from a jar,
  roughly chopped

To finish
75g plain flour
2 large eggs
125g breadcrumbs
Sunflower oil, for frying

To serve
Garlic mayonnaise
Lemon wedges

Start by making the sauce. Heat the butter in a medium saucepan over a medium-high heat until it melts, then stir in the flour using a wooden spoon to make a very thick paste. Allow the paste to cook for a minute until browned slightly. Slowly add the milk, beating constantly – I switch to a whisk when half of the milk is incorporated to ensure there are no lumps. This will be very thick, like porridge without the oats. Reduce the heat to low and cook, stirring for a minute or so, to ensure the starchy taste of the flour is cooked off.

Remove the pan from the heat and stir in the tomato purée, mustard, cheese, cream, chorizo, beans and jalapeños. Pour the mixture onto a plate, cover with clingfilm and refrigerate for at least 3 hours until very stiff – if you have the time and patience, overnight is better.

To assemble, prepare a little production line: put the flour onto a plate, beat the eggs into a bowl and put the breadcrumbs onto another plate. Scoop tablespoons of the chilled filling and shape into chunky pellets – I dip my hands in a little flour to stop the croquettes sticking and roll them into short, fat cylinders. Dust the croquettes in flour, dip them in the egg, then coat them in breadcrumbs. Place the coated croquettes on a plate or tray ready for frying.

Heat 2cm of oil in a large sauté pan or flameproof casserole and allow it to get hot. Fry the croquettes for a minute or so per side until bronzed and crispy – don't overcrowd the pan or the croquettes will never become golden enough, so fry in batches.

Transfer the fried croquettes onto a plate lined with kitchen paper to blot off any excess oil before serving with garlic mayonnaise and lemon wedges.

Deep-frying Option

Although the method above works fine, I do prefer to deep-fry the croquettes to retain their shape. Heat the oil in a deep-fat fryer to 170°C. Once it is hot, add the croquettes in batches, fry until golden, then blot on kitchen paper to remove excess oil before serving.

Make in Advance

The croquettes can be made completely and frozen before cooking. Place them, well spaced, on a baking sheet and freeze. Once they are solid, put into an airtight container or freezer bag and store in the freezer for up to 3 months. The croquettes can be deep-fried from frozen, but will take a little longer at a slightly lower temperature.

something sticky

A Beautiful Mess

*I like the humility and no-fuss nature of sticky
food. Take a lamb chop, for example. It could easily
present itself all aloof, poncily propped upon a
bed of perfectly trimmed vegetables, drizzled with,
and unfulfilled by, some sort of jus. But I'm sure
it would rather accept a little abuse, slathered in
something sticky and flavourful, and be roasted
until tender, demanding you to eat with your fingers.
That's my kind of chop.*

*There's a beauty in the chaotic messiness of it all:
piles of rib bones gnawed by a group of friends,
which clatter as they're thrown down; napkins
stained with sugary stickiness, misshapen and
tossed aside. This kind of jumble exemplifies and
epitomises comfort – feeling eased enough to drop the
facades of fine dining, or the pretence of politeness.
It's primitive, but is modernised with scented
candles and napkins – and probably a dose of
Instagramable food porn.*

*When you eat this food, it sticks so heavily to your
teeth that you're prising it away with your tongue for
hours after the meal is over. This is the kind of fare
that coats your fingers, which you lick frantically,
unashamedly, desperately striving to savour every
morsel. This food is chaotic, but in that lies a deep
calm, the sincerest form of comfort.*

Sticky Fried Lebanese Sprouts

One winter in Manhattan my partner and I did what one does in Manhattan: we mooched and we nibbled. We breathed in the sights of the city, battling the biting chill, and we ate at least five meals a day, telling ourselves it was to give us fuel to combat the startling cold, but we did the same on a summer visit a few years later. One evening we were invited to Ilili, a Lebanese restaurant on 5th Avenue near Madison Square Park. Already absolutely stuffed, we arrived with baggy pants and bold ambition, both much required as the manager continued to bring out plate after plate of awesome Lebanese tapas. The only plate we could finish was, believe it or not, the sprouts. Fried with walnuts, figs and grapes, these were the best sprouts I've ever had. This is my version of them.

SERVES 2–4

75g dried figs,
  finely chopped
75ml dry sherry
200g natural yogurt
1 tbsp finely chopped
  fresh mint
1 tbsp sunflower oil
500g Brussels sprouts,
  trimmed and halved
200g sharp-tasting
  green grapes, halved
75g pecans,
  roughly chopped
½ tbsp sherry vinegar
2 tsp ground sumac
Small handful of
  flat-leaf parsley,
  roughly chopped
Sea salt flakes

Combine the figs and sherry in a small pan and bring to the boil. Boil until the figs cook down and you have a thick paste. Add a splash of water to loosen it into a thick purée. Set aside until needed.

Mix the yogurt with the mint and a pinch of salt. Set aside until needed.

Heat the oil in a decent-sized frying pan over a high heat. Once the oil shimmers from the heat, add the sprouts and fry, tossing frequently, until they smell delightfully nutty and have started to char. Add the grapes and pecans and fry, tossing, for a further minute, then add the sherry vinegar, sumac and parsley and toss together. Finally add the fig purée and toss to combine.

Serve the sprouts on a platter, with the yogurt drizzled over the top.

Miso & Rye Aubergines

The Japanese restaurant Shackfuyu in Soho, London, serves one of the best tasting menus I've had. The fried chicken and the Iberico pork are incredible, but it's simply their humble miso aubergine that draws me in the most. That combination of juicy flesh and the sweet yet oh-so-bold miso just makes my head spin. I added rye whiskey to this, in place of the regular sake, because the whiskey has a fairly similar profile to the miso: full-bodied, a little sweet and most certainly bold. It works beautifully. If you don't have a rye whiskey in, just use regular.

Preheat the oven to 220°C/200°C fan/gas mark 7.

Score deep lines into the flesh of the aubergine about 1cm apart in two directions to crisscross the flesh – be careful not to cut through the skin. Heat a frying pan over a high heat and when it is smoking hot add the aubergines, flesh-side down. Fry the aubergines until the flesh is blackened. If the frying pan isn't large enough, fry the aubergines in batches.

Meanwhile mix together the miso paste, whiskey, honey and sesame seeds. When the aubergines are fried, spread the miso mixture onto the cut surface, working it into the scored cuts. Put the aubergines onto a baking tray and roast for 15–20 minutes, until the paste looks dark and the aubergines look as though they've given up entirely.

To serve, scatter over a little seaweed flakes, if using.

Leftover Ingredient:
Use the leftover miso paste for my Breakfast Ramen on page 46, or Chicken Miso Milanese on page 69.

SERVES 2

2 aubergines,
   halved lengthways
3 tbsp brown rice
   miso paste
2 tbsp rye whiskey
1 tbsp runny honey
1 tsp black sesame seeds

To serve
Dried seaweed flakes
   (I use the brand
   Mara, optional)

Spiced Roasted Monkfish with Sticky Peanut Sauce & Coconut Rice

Monkfish is such a succulent, meaty fish it can take a bit of abuse. It needs to be treated like meat – seared, cooked and rested; but, thanks to its clout, it pairs so well with this sweet, sticky sauce. Be sure to ask your fishmonger to remove that awful thick membrane because, left on, it's a nightmare to eat.

SERVES 4

For the coconut sticky rice
450g jasmine rice
600ml coconut milk
2 kaffir lime leaves (optional)
Fine sea salt and freshly ground black pepper

For the sticky peanut sauce
4 garlic cloves
2 shallots
5cm piece of fresh ginger, peeled
1 lemongrass stalk, tough outer leaves removed
1 tsp dried chilli flakes
2 tsp ground coriander
4 tsp sunflower oil
2 tsp light brown muscovado sugar
1 tsp kecap manis (Indonesian soy sauce)
300g crunchy peanut butter
400ml chicken or vegetable stock
1 tbsp sweet chilli sauce ▶

Before you begin, soak the rice in cold water for at least an hour – a few hours would be even better.

Preheat the oven to 200°C/180°C fan/gas mark 6.

For the peanut sauce, roughly chop the garlic, shallots, ginger and lemongrass and blend in a food processor with the chilli flakes, ground coriander and oil until you have a smooth paste.

Tip the paste into a saucepan, set over a medium heat and gently fry off for 5–10 minutes until the paste is slightly browned and smells strongly. Add the sugar and kecap manis and cook, stirring, for a further 2 minutes. Finally add the peanut butter, stock and sweet chilli sauce, stirring to combine. Bring to the boil and cook for 3–4 minutes until thick and glossy. Set aside until needed.

Drain the rice and put it into a medium saucepan with the coconut milk, lime leaves and a pinch of salt and bring to the boil. Once it is boiling, immediately turn the heat down to low and put a tight-fitting lid on the pan, or cover it with a tea towel before popping on the lid to ensure no steam escapes. Cook over a low heat for 10 minutes. After this time, remove the pan from the heat but don't even think about removing the lid; just allow the rice to steam, covered, in the pan for a further 10 minutes.

Meanwhile, roast the monkfish. Mix together the curry powder, flour and salt and dust the monkfish fillets in this spiced flour.

Heat the oil in a large, heavy-based frying pan over a high heat until it is shimmering. Carefully place the monkfish fillets into the pan and seal off on all sides (about a minute on each) until the flesh is golden and crusty. Transfer the fillets to a roasting tray and roast for 5 minutes in the hot oven. Once cooked, remove the fillets from the oven and rest for 2 minutes. Whilst they are resting you can reheat your sauce and fluff up your rice.

Serve the fish with the coconut sticky rice and the sticky peanut sauce. Garnish with sliced spring onions and chopped roasted peanuts, if that floats your boat.

For the roasted monkfish
4 fillets monkfish (150g each)
4 tbsp curry powder
4 tbsp plain flour
1 tbsp fine sea salt
4 tbsp sunflower oil

To garnish (optional)
3 spring onions, thinly sliced
75g roasted peanuts, roughly chopped

Thai Prawn Sticks

When something is as small as this, the flavour must be intense, strong enough to make up for the wee portion size. The sauce in this recipe uses some powerful ingredients, but with the sweet flesh of the grilled prawns, its sticky kick is welcome. Thai basil adds a more spicy note than the sweet Mediterranean variety and is widely used in Asian dishes as an ingredient rather than simply a garnish.

Skewer 4 prawns onto 4 wooden kebab sticks ready for dipping. Put the garlic, sriracha, soy and fish sauces, honey, lime juice and some of the chopped basil into a small saucepan and mix together. Bring the mixture to the boil, stirring, and allow it to bubble and reduce by half.

Heat a large, dry frying pan over a high heat until very hot. While the pan heats, spread half the sauce over a small plate and set aside. Dip the skewered prawns into the remaining sauce or paint each one with sauce using a small pastry brush.

Fry the sauce-slicked prawn sticks in the dry pan for a minute or so per side, just until the tender flesh is cooked through. Place the prawn sticks on top of the sauce on the plate. Scatter over the remaining chopped Thai basil and serve.

MAKES 4

16 large, uncooked king prawns, peeled and deveined

3 garlic cloves, minced

4 tbsp sriracha (hot chilli sauce)

1 tbsp light soy sauce

2 tsp fish sauce

4 tbsp runny honey

2 tbsp lime juice

Small handful of Thai basil, finely chopped

Lime wedges, to serve

Moroccan Sticky Wings
with Pearled Spelt Pilaf

Pearled spelt is similar to pearl barley, just a bit quicker to cook. You might be surprised at how long the wings are cooked for, but they are a fairly tough cut of chicken, and so need tenderising with a decent stint in the oven. The flavours here are gorgeous. The reduced harissa glaze gives the chicken a sticky spiciness, which balances well with the tender pilaf. The charred lemon refreshes it all, as lemon does, but with a more complex kick.

SERVES 4

1kg chicken wings
1 tbsp olive oil
1 tsp sea salt flakes

For the pilaf
300g pearled spelt
2 tbsp extra virgin
   olive oil
1 red pepper, diced
1 lemon, quartered
½ cucumber, diced
Small handful of
   fresh dill fronds,
   roughly chopped
Small handful of
   fresh mint leaves,
   roughly chopped
250g full-fat
   Greek yogurt
Sea salt flakes

For the glaze
200g rose
   harissa paste
150g runny honey
4 tsp lemon juice

Preheat the oven to 180°C/160°C fan/gas mark 4.

Toss the chicken wings with the oil and salt, then arrange, well spaced, on a baking tray. Transfer to the oven and cook for 45 minutes, until the skin is golden brown and crisp.

Meanwhile, for the pilaf, bring a saucepan of water to the boil. Rinse the pearled spelt in a sieve under cold water and add it to the pan of boiling water. Allow the water to come back to the boil, then reduce to a brisk simmer. Cook the spelt for 20 minutes, or until very fluffy and tender. Drain the spelt in a colander and spread out on a baking sheet to cool evenly.

Heat 1 tablespoon of the oil in a small frying pan over a high heat. Once the oil is hot, add the diced red pepper and fry for a few minutes, stirring, until the pepper is a little softer – though don't completely cook out its texture. Put the pepper into a large bowl. Put the pan back over a high heat and add the quartered lemon. Cook on each side without moving, until the skin is slightly mottled and blackened – a really hot pan is key here. Set the lemon aside until needed.

For the glaze, put the harissa, honey and lemon juice into the same small frying pan and bring to the boil. Reduce to a simmer and cook, stirring frequently, until reduced by half. Remove from the heat and allow to cool.

When the chicken wings have roasted, remove them from the oven and increase the heat of the oven to 240°C/220°C fan/gas mark 8. Coat the wings with the glaze – I find it easiest to put them into a heatproof bowl, add the glaze and mix with a wooden spoon. Put the wings back onto the baking tray and roast for a further 7–10 minutes.

Add the cooled spelt to the bowl containing the cooked
pepper, along with the cucumber, dill, mint, the remaining
olive oil and a pinch of salt. Gently combine everything,
then scatter the pilaf onto a large platter and add the
Greek yogurt in random blobs. Place the chicken wings on
top and finish with the charred lemon quarters.

Balsamic Short Ribs with Cornbread

This is one of those dishes that requires the company and constant use of a damp cloth. If you try to be dainty and eat this with a knife and fork – as David Cameron once did with a hotdog – you'll look daft. This requires a hands-on, almost primitive approach – hence the need for that damp cloth. The ribs are braised in balsamic vinegar then coated in the sticky, reduced liquid and baked with cornbread poured over them.

Preheat the oven to 160°C/140°C fan/gas mark 3.

Heat a large ovenproof saucepan or heavy-based casserole over a high heat. Coat the short ribs with oil and a generous pinch of salt, then fry for a minute or two per side until browned – you may need to do this in batches if the ribs are large. Transfer the ribs to a plate and add the onion, vinegar, sugar, stock, garlic and rosemary to the pan. Allow the mixture to come to the boil and add a pinch of salt and pepper. Return the ribs, cover with a lid and cook in the oven for 2½–3½ hours, until the meat is starting to fall off the bone.

Once the ribs are cooked, remove them from the cooking liquid and set aside. Increase the oven temperature to 200°C/180°C fan/gas mark 6. Bring the cooking liquid to the boil on the hob and allow it to reduce to a thick sauce. Turn the ribs in the sauce to coat, then arrange them snugly on a baking tray and pour over the remaining sauce.

For the cornbread, simply whisk the ingredients to a smooth batter. Pour the cornbread over the ribs and bake for 15 minutes. As soon as the cornbread is set and cakey, serve.

SERVES 2

4 fairly large beef short
  ribs (English cut)
1 tbsp sunflower oil
1 small red onion,
  finely sliced
100ml balsamic vinegar
75g dark brown
  muscovado sugar
400ml beef stock
3 garlic cloves,
  peeled but left whole
2 rosemary sprigs
Fine sea salt and freshly
  ground black pepper

For the cornbread
70g fine cornmeal
140g self-raising flour
½ tsp fine sea salt
½ baking powder
50g Parmesan,
  finely grated
140ml beef stock
1 large egg

Sticky Lamb Stew
with Lager Flatbreads

This was one of the first recipes I wrote for my food blog, over eight years ago. When I changed websites and re-jigged everything, the recipe was lost. Despite trying to re-create it I couldn't quite get the balance right. A few years later, while I was chatting idly to my mum, it transpired she was making it for tea, and had printed the recipe and stashed it amongst her cookery books. This is a dish that suits at any time of year: in the winter, its spiciness gently warms, while in the summer, it is refreshing. The lager is used to make the flatbreads because not only do its bubbles help to aerate the bread, but the fermented, yeast flavour also helps to boost the flavour of the bread.

SERVES 4

3 tbsp olive oil

2 red onions,
    roughly chopped

2 tbsp anchovy paste

2 tbsp tomato purée

4 tsp ras-el hanout

4 preserved lemons,
    finely chopped

4 garlic cloves, minced

4 tsp sherry vinegar
    (or balsamic would do)

2 tsp dried chilli flakes

4 tbsp pomegranate
    molasses

200g dried dates,
    roughly chopped

1kg diced lamb
    (neck, leg or shoulder)

750ml good-quality
    chicken stock

Small handful of
    coriander, chopped

Sea salt flakes and
    coarsely ground
    black pepper ▶

Preheat the oven to 200°C/180°C fan/gas mark 6.

Place a heavy-based ovenproof casserole over a high heat and add the olive oil. Once the oil is hot, add the onions with a pinch of salt and reduce the heat to medium-low. Fry the onions, stirring frequently, for a good 20 minutes. They should soften and colour slightly but not burn.

Once the onions are soft, increase the heat to medium-high and immediately stir in the anchovy paste and tomato purée. Fry, stirring, for a minute, then add the ras-el hanout and stir for a further minute. Add the remaining ingredients except the coriander (no need to brown the lamb) and bring to the boil. Once the stew is boiling, put on a lid and transfer to the oven for 20 minutes, then reduce the temperature to 160°C/140°C fan/gas mark 3. Cook, covered, for 3 hours but do check the casserole halfway through to make sure it isn't too dry – add a splash of water if need be.

Meanwhile, make the flatbreads. Toss the flour, bicarbonate of soda and salt together in a mixing bowl. Pour the lager into the dry ingredients and bring together to form a stiff dough. Turn out onto the worktop and knead for a minute or so, just until smooth. Cover the dough with the upturned mixing bowl and leave to rest for 20 minutes – this will soften the dough, making it easier to roll.

Divide the dough into four portions and roll out each one into a disc about 20cm in diameter. Heat a dry frying pan over a high heat and, once it is hot, fry the flatbreads, one at a time, for 1–2 minutes per side, then flip and fry for a further minute. The flatbreads should swell slightly and be charred. Stack the cooked flatbreads between two plates to keep them soft and warm.

Once the lamb falls apart, it's ready. Sprinkle over the coriander, taste for seasoning, adding salt and pepper if required, and serve with the flatbreads.

For the lager flatbreads

200g strong white
  bread flour
1 tsp bicarbonate
  of soda
1 tsp fine sea salt
120ml lager

Sticky Mongolian Beef Lettuce Cups

I like to think of these as an Eastern fajita, with the lettuce forming a lighter, refreshing version of the tortilla wrap. The beef is sweet, spiced and sticky, and so tender, thanks to the velvet marinade, which includes rice wine - a traditional Chinese technique to ensure meltingly tender meat. The crispy rice adds a wonderful texture to the lettuce cups, so I wouldn't omit that step; though if you're pressed for time you could use a sachet of ready-cooked rice.

Slice the steak into 1cm-thick strips, cutting against the grain of the meat. Mix together the marinade ingredients, add the beef and leave to marinate at room temperature for 30 minutes.

For the crispy rice, heat the oil in a large frying pan on a low-medium heat. Add the rice to the pan and press down flat so it evenly coats the bottom of the pan. Leave the rice to cook, undisturbed, for 5–8 minutes until a golden crust starts to form on the base. Then you can start to move the rice around, frying gently until it is golden and crispy throughout. Mix in the sesame seeds and salt and set aside.

Separate the lettuce leaves – these form your individual 'cups' – give them a quick rinse if they're at all grubby, then pat dry with kitchen paper.

When you're ready to cook the beef, heat the oil in a large frying pan or wok until smoking – you must get the oil violently hot for a stir-fry, otherwise the meat will just become watery and tough. Brown the beef in the oil in batches – it will only take seconds to brown if the oil is hot enough. Use a slotted spoon to remove the beef and set aside on a plate. In the same hot oil fry the garlic, ginger and chilli for 1 minute until they start to brown, then add the soy, water, hoisin and sugar, stirring well to dissolve the mix. Bring to the boil and boil until the mix has reduced and become syrupy – about 3 or 4 minutes. Return the beef to the pan and add the spring onions. Cook over a high heat for a further 2 minutes, ensuring the beef is evenly coated in the rich sticky sauce. Remove from the heat.

Assemble your lettuce cups by filling each with the sticky beef and spring onions and top with crispy sesame rice.

SERVES 4–6

600g beef skirt steak
2 tbsp sunflower oil
3 garlic cloves,
    finely sliced
30g fresh ginger, grated
1 fat red chilli,
    finely chopped
60ml light soy sauce
60ml water
3 tbsp hoisin sauce
60g dark brown
    muscovado sugar
6 spring onions, chopped
    into 2cm pieces
3 Baby Gem lettuces,
    to serve

For the marinade
3 tbsp Shaoxing rice
    wine (or dry sherry)
3 tbsp cornflour
2 tbsp light soy sauce
¼ tsp bicarbonate of soda

For the crispy rice
2 tbsp sunflower oil
250g cold cooked rice
50g toasted sesame seeds
Red chillies, sliced, to serve
Fine sea salt, to taste

Rhubarb & Ginger Jam Lamb Chops with Roasted Potatoes and Beetroot

I can't remember where the inspiration for this recipe came from. I think it was Diana Henry, who, as far as I can recall, posted an Instagram picture from Iceland with a lamb leg cooked in rhubarb jam. Wherever the idea started, I'm sincerely grateful. The mixture of rhubarb and ginger is both tart and warming, which, when married with the earthy beetroot and starchy potato, is just fab.

SERVES 2

500g new potatoes,
  cut into 2cm dice
1 purple beetroot,
  peeled and cut
  into 2cm dice
1 golden beetroot,
  peeled and cut
  into 2cm dice
3 dried bay leaves
1 tbsp olive oil
4 lamb chops
3 tbsp rhubarb
  and ginger jam
Sea salt flakes and
  coarsely ground
  black pepper

Preheat the oven to 220°C/200°C fan/gas mark 7.

Put the potatoes, beetroot and bay leaves into a large roasting dish and toss with the oil and a generous pinch of salt and pepper. Roast for 30 minutes.

Meanwhile rub the lamb chops with the jam, covering the chops completely.

After the vegetables have roasted for 30 minutes, place the lamb chops on top and roast for a further 20 minutes. Remove the dish from the oven, cover it loosely and allow the meat to rest (still on top of everything is fine), for 5 minutes before serving.

Caramel Pork Belly with Sticky Wholegrain Rice

Using sugar in savoury dishes can be dangerous territory: there is the tendency to sprinkle in a teaspoonful or so without rhyme or reason. That sort of practice can end up making a dish unnecessarily sweet. Here, the sugar is first cooked to a deep brown caramel, which develops a depth of flavour that holds its own against the heady spices. I always soak my pork belly in brine overnight. Not only does this help to tenderise the meat and break down the fat, but brining any meat also ensures it remains that bit more juicy when cooked. I wouldn't skip this part.

SERVES 4

Day 1

Mix the ingredients for the brine in a non-metallic bowl or dish and stir until the salt and sugar have dissolved. Add the pork belly, cover with clingfilm and refrigerate overnight.

Day 2

Remove the pork from the brine and dry with kitchen paper. Preheat the oven to 180°C/160°C fan/gas mark 4.

For the sauce, heat a dry ovenproof casserole over a medium-high heat. Once it is hot, add the sugar and allow it to melt and brown into a dark caramel – give the sugar a brief stir if it starts to caramelise unevenly. Throw in the pork belly halves and sear on each side for a minute or so, then add the remaining sauce ingredients with a splash of water. Bring to the boil, cover with a disc of baking paper, then put on a lid and cook in the oven for 2 hours.

Meanwhile, put the rice into a bowl with the bicarbonate of soda and cover with cold water. Leave to soak for an hour, then drain. Put the rice into a saucepan and cover with water by 2cm. Bring the pan to the boil, then reduce the heat to the lowest setting and cover with a lid. Cook for 40–50 minutes, until very sticky – the rice will lose almost all of its texture, but that's what I love.

Serve slices of the pork over bowlfuls of rice.

A Note on Soy

Dark soy sauce is very different from the light variety. The latter is salty and would ruin this recipe. Dark soy sauce is bolder and more treacly, so please don't confuse the two.

1.5kg boneless and
   rindless pork belly,
   cut in two

For the brine
1 litre water
5 tbsp sea salt flakes
1 tbsp caster sugar
1 tbsp coriander seeds
1 tsp whole cloves
2 star anise

For the sauce
100g caster sugar
4 star anise
4 garlic cloves,
   peeled and left whole
3 cloves
1 cinnamon stick
1 fat red chilli,
   halved lengthways
1 tbsp coriander seeds
70ml dark soy sauce
   (see note left)
2 tbsp white wine vinegar

For the rice
200g wholegrain rice
1 tsp bicarbonate of soda

something sticky

something pillowy

Chipper Memories

I spent most of my youth terrorising the local fish and chip shop. My parents owned it, so at weekends I would be cooped up in the back. It was a creaky, cold wooden hut with single-glazed windows and thin walls. But with the fryers fully heated it was, for me, the cosiest place on earth – especially on cold mornings when drops of condensation danced down the windows.

In the corner of the shop was an aluminium steamer set over a gas hob. Its handles hanging off and the sides bashed in from years of use, it stood resilient and towering. Every so often a sharp sputter would break the pre-shift silence, as condensation drizzled down into the flame below. During the hectic Friday night shifts, I would sit quietly (debatable) on the counter, transfixed, as the girls would pluck a pudding from the steamer. They'd toss it from hand to hand, like a hot potato, as they shuffled back to their worktops. There they would invert the pudding, give it a few firm slaps on the base, and remove the foil mould, releasing a cloud of steam.

I was addicted to those steak and kidney puddings, and eating them was a ritual (a daily one during the summer holidays). I'd break the pastry with a sharp chip, dunking it deep into the gravy. Then with a spoon I'd scoop out the filling, sometimes ladling it onto a well-buttered slice of bread or a pile of chips soaked in vinegar. The meat, after hours in the steamer, was flaking and rich. Then, when the suet pastry case was empty, covered in the last traces of meaty gravy, I'd tear off chunks of it, soak them in vinegar, and slowly enjoy the best part of the pudding.

Like most children, increasingly impatient and easily bored, I needed entertainment. Making volcanoes was one of my favourite back-of-house activities: I'd remove the base from a polystyrene chip cone, invert it onto a plate and fill it with scoopfuls of bicarbonate of soda. I'd battle with the huge bottle of vinegar, hauling it across the room, leaving a trail on the tiles. The startling pungency would awaken my nose and make my eyes water as I removed the screw cap. I'd pour the vinegar into my volcano, and as soon as the acid hit the white powder, a mighty, effervescing reaction would cause an explosion of foaming 'lava'. My poor parents would find abandoned volcanoes in every nook and cranny, the culprit evidenced further by empty pudding foils.

Pea and Pie Butties

I couldn't bring myself to devote a page to these ideas, but they are nonetheless extraordinarily good. For the pea butty, a well-buttered barm cake (or bap) is loaded with mushy peas and drenched in vinegar. My sister Jane never seemed to be without a pea butty. Whenever I have it now, I like to take it that step further and add some finely grated piquant cheese – Gruyère is fine.

The pie butty, or Wigan kebab, is a meat and potato pie sandwiched in a buttered barm, slathered with vinegar and brown sauce (or ketchup, depending on your persuasion).

Vietnamese Beef Puddings

This recipe is an ode to that memory and love of steak and kidney pudding in my parents' chippy (see page 114), but it honours my love of spice, too. The steak is slowly cooked in a spiced liquor until it falls apart, before being encased in a tender suet pastry. I would recommend that you serve these with my pickled radishes on page 217 – the sweet and sour counterbalance these gut-busting puddings so well – along with a little wilted pak choi.

MAKES 4

For the filling

3 tbsp sunflower oil

1 red onion,
   finely chopped

1 medium potato, diced

1 carrot, diced

1 celery stick, diced

2 garlic cloves, minced

30g fresh ginger,
   finely grated

1 tbsp plain flour

1 tsp five-spice powder

1 cinnamon stick

1 tsp cardamom pods

3 star anise

2 bay leaves

1 tbsp fish sauce

2 tbsp caster sugar

2 tbsp vinegar
   (any is fine)

400ml beef stock

500g beef skirt
   steak, diced

Fine sea salt and
   coarsely ground
   black pepper

For the pastry

150g shredded beef suet

300g self-raising flour,
   plus extra for dusting

225ml water ▶

Preheat the oven to 160°C/140°C fan/gas mark 3. Grease 4 × 180ml pudding moulds or basins.

For the filling, heat a large casserole over a high heat and add the oil. Once it is hot, add the onion, potato, carrot and celery. Reduce the heat to medium-high and fry for a good 15 minutes, stirring frequently.

Add the garlic, ginger, flour, five-spice, cinnamon, cardamom, star anise, bay and fish sauce and stir. Fry for just a minute, then add the sugar and vinegar, stock and beef. Bring to the boil, pop on a lid and cook in the oven for 3–3½ hours, until the meat is extremely tender and the sauce is thick. Set aside to cool slightly. I always season this after it has cooked; otherwise it so easily becomes too salty because it contains fish sauce. As best you can, remove the cardamom, cinnamon and star anise – I personally don't mind leaving them in, but a few fussy folk may be offended.

For the pastry, simply toss together the suet and flour in a large bowl. Add two-thirds of the water and mix to a dough. If it's a little dry, add a splash more water – the pastry should be soft and pliable but not sticky. Wrap in clingfilm and chill for 30 minutes, or until you're ready to cook.

Preheat the oven to 200°C/180°C fan/gas mark 6.

Lightly dust the worktop with flour and roll out the pastry thinly. Use a plate to cut out four discs big enough to line the pudding moulds – you may need to re-roll the pastry scraps as you go. Leave a little pastry hanging over the edges of the pudding moulds. Fill each pudding mould with the cooled beef filling. Roll out the remaining pastry and cut into discs big enough to top the pies – I use a pint glass as a cutter. Pop the lids on top of the filling and use a fork to crimp the edges together, then trim off any excess pastry. Cut a cross in the top of each pudding to allow steam to escape. There is definitely enough pastry, if you roll it thinly enough. I managed to line two of my tins with one roll, then for the two remaining ones, I had to bundle and re-roll the pastry.

Place the puddings into a roasting tray. Fill the roasting tray with hot water (from the hot tap is fine) so that it comes halfway up the sides of the pudding moulds. Cover the roasting tray with clingfilm, then with foil. Bake for 35 minutes and serve immediately with the optional radishes and pak choi.

Leftover Filling
There will possibly be a little filling left over: don't throw it away. It is delicious on top of a jacket potato, or even on a slab or two of sourdough toast.

To serve (optional)
Anise and Bay
  Pickled Radishes
  (see page 217)
Stir-fried pak choi

something pillowy

Veggie Burgers & Purple Fries

A real burger, drenched in meaty juices that seep down and soak the bottom half of the bun, is a difficult thing to contend with; there's little more satisfying when feasting than meaty juices trickling down your chin. But I find veggie burgers, done well, to be so fulfilling. Not only do you get that mouthful of good, hearty grub, but also you feel as though you're getting so much nourishment with each bite. And if you can't be without meat, do what I do and add a slice of bacon or two – it's a revelation. The purple sweet potato fries are just to add a little colour – if you can't get hold of them, use the more common orange variety.

Put the sweet potato fries in a bowl and cover with cold water. Leave to soak until required – this will help to draw out some of the starch that prevents the fries from crisping up.

Put the quinoa into a sieve and run under cold water until the water runs clear. Put the quinoa into a saucepan with 300ml water and a very generous pinch of salt. Bring to the boil, then reduce to a simmer and cook for 20 minutes, or until the quinoa is soft and the water is fully absorbed. Set aside to cool to room temperature.

Mash the cannellini beans with a fork, then add to a bowl with the cooled quinoa, the grated parsnip, breadcrumbs, coriander, egg and a generous pinch of salt and pepper. Mix together to form a thick paste. Form into four large balls, pat them down into burgers and place on a tray – I wrap a plastic chopping board in clingfilm. Pop the burgers into the fridge to chill and firm for 30 minutes or so.

Preheat the oven to 200°C/180°C fan/gas mark 6.

Drain the sweet potato and dry with a clean tea towel. Put them into a large sandwich bag or bowl and toss together with the paprika, garlic salt and cornflour. Spread out, well spaced, on a baking tray and bake for 20–25 minutes, or until crisp.

For the burgers, heat a generous glug of sunflower oil in a frying pan over a high heat. Once the oil is hot, reduce the heat to medium and add the burgers. Fry for 5–7 minutes on each side until golden brown and crispy – flipping them shouldn't be too difficult; these are firmer than most crumbling veggie burgers.

Assemble the burgers in their buns with the other serving suggestions however you fancy them – I mix the mayo and harissa and spread that on the buns before piling in the rest. Serve the fries alongside.

MAKES 4

For the fries
2 large purple sweet
  potatoes, peeled
  and cut into fries
1 tsp paprika
½ tsp garlic salt
1 tsp cornflour

For the burgers
150g black quinoa
300ml water
400g can cannellini
  beans, drained
1 parsnip, finely grated
75g breadcrumbs
Small handful of coriander,
  finely chopped
1 medium egg
Sunflower oil, for frying
Fine sea salt and freshly
  ground black pepper

To serve
4 brioche buns
6 tbsp mayonnaise
1 tbsp rose harissa
Coleslaw (shop-bought
  or use my recipe
  on page 215)
Small handful of
  coriander leaves
1 beef tomato, sliced

something pillowy

Poppyseed & Caraway Bagels

Real, homemade, bagels are unrivalled. They are nothing like the mass-produced shop-bought varieties that come piled high and shrouded in impersonal, corporate plastic. These have a chewiness but, when fresh, are soft enough to eat without toasting. They cry out to be converted into smoked salmon bagels with cream cheese, cucumber slices and tangy capers; though of course, the salt beef on page 167 would also be a very welcome filling.

MAKES 12

For the dough

500g strong white
    bread flour
1½ tsp fine sea salt
1 tbsp caster sugar
7g sachet fast-
    action yeast
1 tbsp sunflower oil
240ml water
1 large egg

To finish

3 tbsp poppy seeds
1 tbsp caraway seeds
1 egg, beaten

For the dough, put all the ingredients into a large mixing bowl and mix to a stiff dough. Turn out onto a floured worktop and knead for 10 minutes, or until smooth and elastic. Alternatively use a mixer fitted with a dough hook for 5 minutes.

Divide the dough into 12 equal portions, roll each one into a neat ball and place on a floured chopping board. Cover with oiled clingfilm and set aside to prove for 30 minutes, or until the dough has doubled in size.

When the dough has doubled in size, make a hole in the centre of each ball using a wooden spoon, stretching the hole with your fingers so it doesn't reseal. Cover the bagels and set aside for 30 minutes, to prove a second time, until they feel aerated and soft – don't manhandle them too much, or they'll deflate.

Preheat the oven to 230°C/210°C fan/gas mark 8.

Bring a large saucepan of water to a simmer, add the bagels in batches (taking care not to overcrowd the pan) and poach for 1 minute per side. Scoop the bagels out with a slotted spoon and place on a cooling rack to dry slightly. At this stage the bagels will look like deflated, moist rings but, don't worry, they'll puff up beautifully in the oven. Scatter the seeds onto a plate. Glaze the bagels with beaten egg, then dip the glazed side into the seeds.

Line two baking sheets with baking paper. Place the poached bagels on the baking sheets with plenty of room between them and bake in the oven. After 10 minutes, swap the position of the sheets in the oven and bake for a further 5 minutes. Allow the bagels to cool on a wire rack, then store in an airtight tin. They'll be fresh enough for a day or two, but thereafter a brief stint in the toaster will revive them.

Mushroom, Spinach & Ricotta Yorkshire Pudding

This is something of a cross between pizza and toad in the hole, with my favourite ravioli filling on top. The key to the Yorkshire pudding is to ensure the pan is ferociously hot before you pour in the batter; otherwise you'll just end up with something that resembles a rubbery bathmat.

Preheat the oven to 250°C/230°C fan/gas mark 9. For the batter, put the oil into the base of a medium roasting dish (about 30×20cm) and put into the oven to get very hot.

To make the batter, put the milk and eggs into a jug and beat together. Toss the flour and salt in a bowl and add a generous splash of the liquid ingredients. Whisk to form a smooth, thick batter, then slowly pour in the remaining liquid, whisking as you go. By this time the oil should have got very hot in the roasting tray, so drop a little of the batter in – if it sizzles, the oil is ready. If not, leave the tray in the oven until it is hot. Pour the batter into the tray and return it to the oven. Bake for 20–25 minutes, until the Yorkshire pudding has puffed up and is deep golden around the edges.

Meanwhile, make the filling. Heat a dry frying pan over a high heat and add the spinach. Cook, stirring, until the spinach wilts down, then tip it into a sieve set over a bowl. Add the oil, butter, mushrooms and onion to the pan and cook, stirring frequently, until the mushrooms soften and colour – you need to ensure all excess liquid has evaporated from the pan. Remove the pan from the heat.

Squeeze the excess moisture out of the spinach and discard its liquid. Put into a bowl with the mushrooms and onions and add the nutmeg, ricotta and pecorino cheese. Season to taste.

When the Yorkshire pudding is golden and puffed, remove it from the oven and scatter the filling over it – you might need to press the pudding down in the centre if it has ballooned up completely. Scatter the torn mozzarella on top of the filling. Return the tray to the oven for 10–15 minutes, until the mozzarella cheese has melted. Serve immediately.

SERVES 4

For the batter

2 tbsp sunflower oil

225ml full-fat milk

4 large eggs

115g self-raising flour

½ tsp fine sea salt

For the filling

400g spinach, washed

1 tbsp sunflower oil

50g unsalted butter

400g chestnut mushrooms, finely sliced

1 small onion, finely sliced

¼ tsp freshly grated nutmeg

250g ricotta

125g pecorino cheese, finely grated

100g mozzarella, torn into small pieces

Fine sea salt and coarsely ground black pepper

Sweet Potato Gnocchi with Amaretti & Brown Butter

Squash and amaretti may seem a strange combination to us Brits, but the pairing is quite a common ravioli or tortelli filling in Emilia Romagna, northern Italy. The flavour is intensely autumnal, especially with the addition of nutty brown butter and sage. Making gnocchi isn't at all difficult; it's just like making bread dough without the vigorous kneading. The shaping to achieve the ridges is fiddly at first, but you'll soon develop a rhythm; however, it isn't totally necessary – you could use the pillow shapes cut from the sausages of dough. The most beautiful thing about this dish, apart from the eating, is how the colour of the gnocchi transforms the more you cook it. When first mixed, it's a muted orange. When blanched, it becomes a little more vibrant, and then, when fried, the colour is gorgeously rich.

For the gnocchi

500g sweet potato
(about 2), whole
and unpeeled
200g–250g '00'
pasta flour
50g unsalted butter
1 tbsp olive oil
Sea salt flakes

To serve

150g butter
12 fresh sage leaves
2 amaretti biscuits,
crumbled

Preheat the oven to 200°C/180°C fan/gas mark 6.

Place the sweet potatoes on a baking sheet and cover them generously with salt – this will help to draw out some of the moisture. Roast the potatoes for 1 hour, or until the insides feel mushy when you squeeze them – do so carefully, they'll obviously be bloody hot. Allow the potatoes to cool until you can handle them then squeeze the flesh into a mixing bowl and discard the skins.

Add a pinch of salt to the sweet potato and mix in thoroughly, mashing the potato well. Now add the pasta flour, a heaped tablespoon at a time, mixing well after each addition. As the mixture gets thicker, you'll need to squeeze it together with your hands. As soon as you have a smooth dough that is stiff but malleable, it's ready – you might need more flour than stated here.

Divide the dough in half and roll into two very long sausages between 60 and 70cm in length. Using a sharp knife cut each sausage into 2cm pillows. To give the gnocchi their classic ridged surface, place each pillow lengthways across a fork, cut-side against the tines. Squash the pillow onto the fork using your index finger, applying just enough pressure to leave an indentation. Then roll the gnocchi off the fork – it should curl up around that indentation, achieving the characteristic rounded, bullet shape with a seam at the back. Place the gnocchi onto a lightly floured surface until required.

Blanching the gnocchi will help to prevent them from becoming soggy when they are fried: bring a saucepan of well-salted water to the boil, and have a bowl of iced water ready. Drop the gnocchi into the boiling

water and cook for 2 minutes – usually gnocchi float to the surface, but sweet potato gnocchi can be a little denser. Scoop the gnocchi out of the pan and drop them into the iced water, then spread out on a cooling rack or plate.

Place a frying pan over a medium-high heat and add the 50g butter with a tablespoon of oil. When the butter has melted, add the gnocchi and fry for 2–3 minutes until golden brown, then turn them over – just give the pan a gentle shimmy, or use kitchen tongs – and fry until golden brown and crisp on the other side.

Tip the gnocchi onto a plate. Don't bother to wipe the pan out; just set it over a medium-high heat and add the 150g butter. When the butter melts, gently swirl it around in the pan allowing the milk solids to brown on the bottom. A fine cappuccino-like foam should form, and the butter should smell intensely nutty. Add the gnocchi back to the pan, along with the sage leaves, and toss to coat in the butter. Serve with a light sprinkling of amaretti.

something pillowy

Spelt Dough Balls with Beef Dripping Garlic Butter

Dough balls, however sophisticated or unsophisticated you make them, epitomise that pillowy comfort that we all crave from time to time. These, slathered in a hot mixture of butter and beef dripping, are pure filth. I think they work especially well dunked into a baked wheel of Camembert (just slash the top of a wheel, in the bottom half of its wooden box, and bake in a hot oven until molten and bubbling – about 15 minutes).

To make the dough, put the flours, yeast, sugar and salt into a mixing bowl and add most of the water. Bring together into a scraggy dough – it will of course be sticky, but don't go adding more flour in fright because you'll only dry it out. Work the dough, stretching it and slapping it about, until it becomes elastic and smooth. You can either do this in a mixer fitted with a dough hook attachment and it will take about 5 minutes, or 10 minutes kneading by hand. Put the dough into a greased bowl and cover with clingfilm. Allow to rise until doubled in size – this might take an hour or even longer depending on the temperature of the room.

Once the dough has risen, weigh the bulk of the dough and that number by 24. Portion the dough into 24 equal amounts, weighing each for precision. Roll each portion of dough into a neat ball, then place in a large, deep-sided roasting tray, leaving a little space between each ball. Allow to prove until swollen and the balls are touching one another.

Preheat the oven to 220°C/200°C fan/gas mark 7.

Once the dough balls have proved, bake them for 10–12 minutes, or until lightly golden and slightly crispy, but with a supple bounce to them.

Meanwhile, put the butter, dripping, garlic and thyme into a saucepan over a medium heat until melted. Leave over a medium heat for a good 5 minutes or so to infuse and soften the tang of the garlic. Once the dough balls come out of the oven, pour over the butter and dripping mixture and sprinkle with sea salt flakes. Serve from the roasting tray.

MAKES 24

For the dough
300g white bread flour
200g spelt flour
7g sachet fast-
  action yeast
1 tsp caster sugar
10g fine sea salt
325–350ml water

For the beef dripping garlic butter
125g salted butter
125g beef dripping
3 garlic cloves,
  finely sliced
Leaves from 6 thyme
  sprigs, chopped
Sea salt flakes

Greek Salad Frittata

My dad once took me on a father-son holiday to Crete. For two weeks we had the best adventure, driving around the island. We'd eat fresh fish and dance in the tavernas, red-cheeked from wine and sun.

On a visit to the ancient city of Lato, the wind was warm and wild as we climbed the hill, and something blew into my eye. I chicken-scratched desperately to get the morsel out, but it was stuck fast. The agony was unbearable. My dad drove us to the nearby town of Kritsa where I washed my eye in the fountain of the town square. After I had furiously thrashed the water to my face, the speck of dust surrendered, and we celebrated by eating in the closest restaurant – a little taverna with gingham tablecloths. We had omelettes and Greek salad, washed down with red wine. Whenever I make this frittata, I look fondly on that moment.

SERVES 4–6

12 eggs, separated
2 tbsp olive oil
1 red onion, chopped
1 green pepper, diced
1 red pepper, diced
1 garlic clove,
    finely chopped
300ml whipping cream
250g cherry tomatoes,
    halved
80g pitted Kalamata
    olives, halved
100g feta
2 tbsp fresh oregano,
    chopped
Small handful of
    flat-leaf parsley,
    roughly chopped
1 tsp red wine vinegar
1 tbsp extra virgin
    olive oil
Sea salt flakes and
    coarsely ground
    black pepper

Preheat the oven to 200°C/180°C fan/gas mark 6.

Whisk the egg whites in a spotlessly clean bowl to soft peaks, then set aside.

Heat a large, deep-sided (preferably non-stick) ovenproof frying pan over a medium-high heat. Add the olive oil and red onion and cook for 2 minutes or so, until the onion starts to soften. Add the green and red pepper and garlic and cook for a further 4–5 minutes, until the peppers soften and the garlic smells strongly.

While the peppers are cooking, give the egg whites another whisk to bring them back together. Add the eggs yolks, cream, salt and pepper to the bowl and whisk to combine.

Turn the oven temperature down to 180°C/160°C fan/gas mark 4 and turn on the grill element to medium heat – or, if you can't use the grill function at the same time as the oven, preheat the grill to medium-high.

Add half of the cherry tomatoes, the olives, feta and oregano to the pan, while still over a medium-high heat. Stir well, then pour in the egg mixture. Cook until the eggs just begin to set. Remove from the heat and place on a high shelf in the oven. Cook for 5 minutes.

Meanwhile, put the remaining cherry tomatoes in a small bowl. Add the parsley, vinegar and oil. Season with salt and pepper and stir well.

Remove the frittata from the oven and allow it to sit for 2 minutes. Transfer the frittata from the pan to a serving dish and top with the tomatoes to serve.

Fish Pie Potato Skins

When you consider the essential properties of a fish pie – wholesome, comforting, nourishing – it seems a shame that most recipes discard the potato skins, which are not only packed with so many nutrients but also delicious. That really is the provenance of this recipe.

As with most comfort foods, there are countless versions of fish pie, each personal to its creator. Some use a béchamel sauce, others use a wine, stock and cream reduction. Here I find crème fraîche works a treat, not merely because it's a darn sight quicker than all other options, but also because its thickness means that it won't seep out of the potato skins too much should there be a slight hole.

Preheat the oven to 210°C/190°C fan/gas mark 7. Put the potatoes on a baking tray and bake for 1–1½ hours, until the skins are crispy and the insides soft. Remove from the oven and allow to cool until you can handle them. Reduce the temperature to 200°C/180°C fan/gas mark 6.

Heat the butter in a frying pan over a medium heat. Once the butter melts, add the leek and fry until very soft – about 20 minutes – stirring occasionally. Put the leek into a bowl with the remaining filling ingredients and stir to mix well.

Halve the potatoes and scoop most of the flesh into a bowl – leave about 5mm of flesh against the skin. Fill each potato skin with the fish filling and place on a baking tray – or use a 12-hole bun tin so the filled potato halves don't fall over.

Add the topping ingredients to the bowl of potato and mix until fairly smooth, then blob it on top of the fish filling in each potato skin. Bake for 20–30 minutes, until the potato is slightly coloured.

SERVES 6

6 medium
  baking potatoes

For the filling
40g unsalted butter
1 leek, very finely sliced
2 anchovies,
  finely chopped
100g skinless salmon,
  cut into 1cm cubes
100g skinless pollack,
  cut into 1cm cubes
100g skinless smoked
  haddock, cut into
  1cm cubes
200g crème fraîche
1 tbsp finely chopped
  flat-leaf parsley
1 tbsp finely chopped
  fresh chives
1 tbsp wholegrain mustard
1 tsp fine sea salt
1 tsp black pepper

For the topping
1 tsp fine sea salt
50g Gruyère, finely grated
1 tbsp crème fraîche

something pillowy

131

Pork Potsticker Dumplings

Potstickers are dumplings with crispy bases. They are fried briefly before and after steaming which gives them their characteristic golden-brown bottoms. Their provenance, as with tarte Tatin, lies in serendipity – or idle-mindedness: a Chinese chef in the process of boiling dumplings became distracted and wandered off. While he was absent, the water in the wok boiled away and the dumplings stuck to the wok. They became charred and crisp on the bottom. The potsticker dumpling was born.

MAKES 16

For the dough

100g high-gluten
  dumpling flour (or
  strong white bread
  flour would work)
50ml (approx.)
  boiling water

For the filling

175g pork mince
1 spring onion,
  finely sliced
½ tsp bicarbonate
  of soda
½ tsp cornflour
2 tsp light soy sauce
2 tsp dark soy sauce
1 tsp toasted
  sesame oil
Pinch of fine sea salt
½ tsp white pepper

Sunflower oil, for
  greasing and frying ▸

For the dough, mix together the flour and the water until you have a firm but soft dough – you may need to add a little more water if it's dry, but this shouldn't be wet or sticky. Knead for about 2 minutes, until smooth, then form into a ball. Cover with greased clingfilm and set aside to rest for about 20 minutes.

Stir together the filling ingredients in a bowl until evenly mixed.

Divide the dough into 16 even portions. Lightly flour the worktop and roll out each portion to form a disc about 8cm in diameter.

Take a heaped teaspoon of the filling and put into the centre of each disc. Seal – you can twist the dough into little 'money parcels', which is easier, or pleat them: fold the dough over the filling to create a half-moon shape. Pinch the edge to seal, then pleat. The most difficult way, but the way I prefer (pictured), is the Nepalese method: holding the disc of dough in your non-dominant hand, pile the filling into the centre of the dough. With your right hand (or left) make three pleats in the dough on one side, then fold this pleated edge up and over to the centre of the filling. With your right index finger and thumb, seal the dumpling, bringing in the dough from its left and right edge. Seal the end by rolling it into a point. Store uncooked dumplings on a well-greased tray covered with a clean, damp cloth – you don't want them drying out.

Heat a little oil in a lidded frying pan over a medium-high heat. When the oil is hot, add the dumplings and fry until golden brown on the bottom – about 2 minutes. Pour in 50ml water and cover with a lid. Steam, without lifting the lid, for 3 minutes, then uncover the pan and fry for a further minute to crisp up the bottom of the dumplings.

For the sauce, simply mix together the soy, chilli and sesame oil, and pour it onto a shallow bowl. Serve the dumplings with the sauce on the side and scatter over the coriander and spring onion.

For the sauce

3 tbsp dark soy sauce

2 tbsp finely chopped
  red chilli or
  lazy chilli from a jar

2 tbsp toasted sesame oil

To serve

Coriander leaves,
  roughly chopped

1 spring onion,
  very finely sliced

Pork Bao Buns

I have a particular obsession with food encased in parcels – it must stem from my Lancashire upbringing: pies were, and still are, a staple. But when it comes to this kind of food, a steamed pork bun takes some beating – not that I wish to shun the food of my heritage, but surely everyone craves the exotic and otherworldly from time to time? Bao buns are pillowy, they stick to your teeth a little, and their filling screams with flavour. Usually the bread part is made with yeast, but I've made things a lot simpler here: baking powder gives just as good a result, and it's far quicker. Steam them in deep-sided paper muffin cases.

First make the dough. Put the flour, baking powder and sugar into a mixing bowl and toss together. Put the salt in a jug with the milk and stir to dissolve, then add to the flour and bring together into a smooth dough – I use my hands, but feel free to use a wooden spoon. Once the dough has come together, tip onto the worktop and knead very briefly just until smooth. If the dough is a little sticky, add a small amount of flour, but don't overdo it. Return the dough to the bowl and leave to rest while you make the filling.

For the filling, just mix everything together in a bowl – I use my hands to make sure everything is perfectly combined.

Divide the dough into 8 equal balls. Lightly flour the worktop and roll out each ball to form a disc about 8cm in diameter. Put a heaped teaspoon of filling into the centre of each disc, then bring the edges of dough up over the filling, pinching to seal.

Set a bamboo steamer (or whatever type you have) over a pan of boiling water. Grease 8 deep muffin cases with a little oil and put the buns, seam-side down, into the cases. Set the muffin cases into the steamer, pop on the lid, and cook for 12–15 minutes, until the buns are puffed up and hot to the touch. Allow to cool slightly and serve.

MAKES 8

For the dough

250g low-gluten bun
   flour (or plain flour)
2 tsp baking powder
2 tsp caster sugar
1 tsp sea salt flakes
170ml full-fat milk

For the filling

150g pork mince
1 carrot, coarsely grated
1 tbsp hoisin sauce
1 tbsp oyster sauce
1 tbsp light soy sauce
1 red chilli, deseeded
   and finely chopped
1 spring onion,
   finely chopped
Small handful of
   coriander, finely
   chopped

Midnight French Toast

French toast – eggy bread as I fondly call it – is a source of almost instant gratification: bung a few ingredients into a bowl, whisk, dunk, fry, and you've got a breakfast dish that dreams are made of. Ordinarily, it's slathered with maple syrup or sugar, but I prefer something a little more sophisticated, so this version is made with treacle and liquorice powder. Those dark components are what the title refers to: the sauce becomes so blackened and glossy that it reminds me of a satiny midnight sky.

MAKES 4 SLICES

For the sauce
300g blueberries
2 tbsp black treacle
2 tbsp caster sugar
1 tbsp lemon juice
1 tsp liquorice
  powder (I use the
  Swedish brand
  Lakritsfabriken)

For the toast
2 large eggs
150ml milk
1 tbsp black treacle
1 tsp vanilla extract
4 thick slices of bread
  (I use brioche,
  but regular bread
  works too)
50g unsalted butter
  for frying, plus
  extra to serve
Icing sugar, to serve

First make the sauce. Put all the ingredients into a saucepan and set over a high heat. As the blueberries cook they will break down slightly and release their juice. Boil the sauce for 3–4 minutes, stirring occasionally, until the fruits are broken down and the sauce is a little thicker. Remove from the heat.

For the toast, beat together the eggs, milk, treacle and vanilla in a jug until well mixed, then pour onto a plate or shallow dish. Dip the slices of bread into the egg – I flip them four times in the mixture.

Heat a medium frying pan over a high heat and add the butter. As soon as the butter starts to bubble, reduce the heat to medium-low and add the egg-soaked bread – I fry two pieces at a time. Fry about 3–5 minutes, until the underside is mottled and dark golden brown, then flip and fry until the other side matches.

To serve, stack the toast onto a plate. Add a knob of butter, then pour over that midnight black sauce. Finish with a light dusting of icing sugar and serve.

something tender

Warm of Heart

The Italians have a saying: 'a tavola non s'invecchia' – at the table nobody grows old. For me, this doesn't mean that sitting down to eat with the family is an elixir of eternal youth – with my family and our bickering, I think I age 10 years at every meal. Instead, the proverb epitomises how sweet the air can be when we sit down together with good food and wine – so sweet that the hours just dance away. No one notices how late it gets; no one looks on it as wasted time. I like to think, too, that laughing, even debating passionately, with our kinfolk is a recalibration of our values and the things that matter to us.

But my guess is that, for many of us, the ideal of a family crowded table is no more than memory (if not, then cling to it for as long as you can). With increasing pressure to work, earn, sleep, repeat, time together is sacrificed. From a personal point of view, the Sundays that used to be filled with little more than feasting with my clan now merge into the rest of the week. If I'm not scrubbing my cookery school floor, or testing recipes for new classes, I'm just arsing about in the kitchen – I don't berate it, I love my job. But once in a while my mind flickers to a crowded table, fighting to eat the crispiest potatoes and the pink-centred slices of roast beef; hands from all directions snaffling spuds and sharing sauces.

Every time we eat, and how we eat, landmarks where we are in our personal lives. If you're so busy that you guzzle a packet sandwich at your desk, or skip lunch entirely, can you really say that you are caring for yourself? I found myself eating lunch standing up recently. I stopped, mid-forkful, alone but embarrassed by the image: a 27-year-old slouched against the worktop with terrible posture and uncombed hair. I'd become a slob. Not a lazy slob, plonked on the couch, ordering takeaway for lunch, but I was lazy with myself for the 'greater good' of industry. I took the full hour to eat, stroll and think. I got much more done that afternoon.

It may seem a cliché, but food that is cooked with a full heart is the best. Whenever I teach a bread class I always tell my students that if the dough is made with anger, the result is heavy and dense – a deadweight. When made with love and warmth of heart, the bread is perfect. That rings true in all cookery, too: the cuts of meat that require, and receive, a softer approach become the most tender. My mother's cooking isn't technically advanced, but that doesn't matter. Nothing will ever compete with it, because what she produces is food cooked with love: love for the ingredients and love for the eaters.

This isn't just about respect for the ingredients. We owe it to ourselves to nurture and nourish ourselves with a warm heart.

Lemon & Pea Pearl Barley Risotto with Twice-marinated Feta

The most comforting thing about a risotto is the combination of satisfying smoothness and the texture of the grains. With pearl barley, that is amplified: a bigger grain means a bigger bite with every mouthful.

You may think it odd to soak the feta in milk, but it's a wonderful thing. The milk draws out that startling saltiness, which means you can taste the complex creaminess of the feta. But that salt isn't wasted; the milk is added to the risotto at the end, boosting both flavour and feel.

Put the stock, half the peas, the 3 strips of lemon zest and the crushed garlic into a pan and bring to the boil. Simmer for 5 minutes, then set aside to cool. Once the mixture has cooled, blitz in a blender to a smooth liquid.

Heat a generous glug of olive oil in a large, shallow casserole over a medium-high heat and, once it is hot, add the spring onions with a pinch of salt. Fry, stirring occasionally, for 3–4 minutes, then add the pearl barley, the stock mixture, the lemon juice and the reserved peas. Bring to the boil, reduce to a simmer and cook for 40–45 minutes, stirring frequently. If the risotto starts to look dry, add a little water.

Meanwhile, chop the feta into small chunks and add to a bowl along with the milk. Leave to sit for 15 minutes, then drain (reserve the milk). Put the feta into a bowl with the remaining lemon zest, mint and extra virgin olive oil with a pinch of pepper. Leave to marinate while the risotto cooks.

Once the pearl barley is tender, it's ready. Add the reserved milk to the risotto, stirring until completely combined. Turn off the heat, test for seasoning and stir through the parsley. Serve, topped with the feta.

SERVES 4

1 litre good-
  quality chicken
  or vegetable stock
300g frozen peas
Zest and juice of 1
  unwaxed lemon (use a
  potato peeler to remove
  3 strips of zest, scraping
  off any white pith with
  a knife, and reserve
  the rest for the feta)
3 garlic cloves, minced
Olive oil
6 spring onions,
  finely chopped
400g pearl barley, rinsed
Small handful of flat-leaf
  parsley, roughly chopped
Sea salt flakes and coarsely
  ground black pepper

For the marinated feta
200g feta
200ml milk
Remaining zest from
  the lemon
10 mint leaves,
  very finely chopped
50ml extra virgin olive oil

something tender

Roasted Jerusalem Artichoke & Smoked Garlic Soup

Jerusalem artichokes are strange nuggets. They're not actually artichokes at all, but tubers, related to sunflowers; moreover, they are not from Jerusalem, but the name is a corruption of the Italian word 'girasole' meaning sunflower. Their appearance is dour, but their taste is sweet, nutty and earthy, and pairs perfectly with smoked garlic.

As with any garlic, the smoked version loses its acrid taste and becomes sweet and quietly confident when roasted. If you can't find smoked, regular garlic is just fine, but that subtle campfire scent that the smoked version brings is incomparable.

SERVES 4–6

1kg Jerusalem artichokes
2 smoked garlic bulbs
2 tbsp sunflower oil
50g unsalted butter
1 large onion,
   finely chopped
1 litre vegetable stock
Sea salt flakes and
   coarsely ground
   white pepper
Runny honey, to serve

Preheat the oven to 200°C/180°C fan/gas mark 6.

Peel the artichokes and chop larger ones to match the size of the smaller ones. Put them into a roasting tray and drizzle over most of the oil. Halve the garlic bulbs horizontally, rub them with the remaining oil, and individually wrap them in foil. Put them in the roasting tray with the artichokes and roast everything for 45 minutes, until the artichokes are soft to the touch.

Meanwhile, heat a large saucepan over a medium heat. Add the butter to the pan and, once it melts, add the onion. Reduce the heat to low and fry for 25–30 minutes, stirring occasionally, until the onion is very soft and translucent. Add the roasted artichokes to the pan. Squeeze the garlic, which will have turned almost to a paste, from the skin and add it to the pan. Add the stock and bring to the boil, then turn off the heat and blitz, either in a food processor or using a stick blender, to a smooth soup. If the soup is a little thick, thin it out with water.

Season to taste and serve with a drizzle of honey on top.

Aubergine, Courgette & Halloumi Bake

I wish I could wax lyrical about how beautiful a place Cyprus is and how it inspired this dish, but I've never been. My only taste of Cyprus is literally just that – a taste. And, unsurprisingly, it starts with halloumi cheese and oregano. Halloumi is a firm favourite of mine. Chewed squeakily in its raw form, it is meaty and salty. Cooked, it yields to the heat, softening, but retains a firmness that isn't matched by that of many other cheeses. Oregano is a perfect pairing, with its assertive herbal mustiness, not too dissimilar to marijuana. The dried form is so over-used by cheap Italian restaurants, but don't let that put you off: fresh oregano is heaven-sent and heaven-scented.

Heat a sauté pan or deep-sided frying pan over a medium-high heat and add the oil. Once it is hot, add the onion and cook, stirring frequently, until it is soft and slightly coloured – about 15 minutes.

Stir in the garlic and tomatoes and allow to cook until the tomatoes mush down and become a little cloudy. Increase the heat to high, add the wine and allow it to bubble and almost entirely evaporate, then add the stock. Once the stock comes to the boil, remove the pan from the heat and stir in the oregano, and salt and pepper to taste – remember that the aubergine and courgette will dilute the flavour, so make it ever so slightly salty.

Preheat the oven to 200°C/180°C fan/gas mark 6.

Put the diced aubergines and courgette into a roasting dish with the olives and mix together. Pour over the sauce and bake for 30 minutes, then lay the halloumi slices on top and return to the oven for a further 15 minutes, until the sauce is bubbling and the halloumi pieces are slightly charred.

Serve with torn chunks of bread.

SERVES 4–6

3 tbsp olive oil
1 large onion, finely sliced
3 garlic cloves, minced
400g fresh vine tomatoes, roughly chopped
175ml dry white wine
200ml strong vegetable stock
Small handful of fresh oregano leaves, roughly chopped
2 medium aubergines, cut into 2cm dice
1 large courgette, cut into 2cm dice
100g pitted black olives, roughly chopped
250g block halloumi, finely sliced
Sea salt flakes and coarsely ground black pepper
Crusty white bread, to serve

One-pot Tarragon Chicken, Mushrooms & Rice

Tarragon was made for chicken and mushrooms. Its muted aniseed flavour is somehow both bold and gentle; the sponginess of the mushrooms just soaks up the tarragon and their earthiness marries with it beautifully. The second wonder of this dish is its simplicity – just throw everything into the pan, place the chicken on top and roast.

Preheat the oven to 200°C/180°C fan/gas mark 6.

Put the chicken stock and wine into a large, shallow ovenproof casserole and bring to the boil. Put the rice into a sieve and rinse under the cold tap until the water runs clear.

When the liquid is boiling, add the rice, mushrooms, shallot and tarragon with a pinch of salt and pepper and stir to combine. Place the thighs, skin-side up, on top, drizzle them with oil and sprinkle over a little salt and pepper. Cook in the oven, uncovered, for 45–50 minutes, until the chicken is deeply bronzed and the rice is tender. Serve immediately.

SERVES 4

800ml chicken stock
150ml dry white white
225g basmati rice
200g mixed mushrooms, finely sliced
1 banana shallot, finely sliced
2 tbsp finely chopped fresh tarragon leaves
6–8 chicken thighs
Olive oil
Sea salt flakes and freshly ground black pepper

Lamb & Black Olives in Rosé Wine with Wholewheat Pasta

While the idea of pasta often conjures up something speedy, there's little that can beat a slow-cooked pasta sauce. Whenever I cook with lamb I try to use anchovies, which really enhance the flavour of the meat. The result of the slow cooking and the anchovies is a sauce so seriously savoury that a little goes a long way. On that note, don't forget to reserve the pasta cooking water to let the sauce down a little – that's the key to achieving a sauce that is rich, but not overpowering.

SERVES 4

For the pasta
400g dried wholewheat
    pappardelle
75ml extra virgin olive
    oil (I prefer Ligurian)
Small handful of
    flat-leaf parsley,
    roughly chopped

For the sauce
50g unsalted butter
1 tbsp sunflower oil
1 onion, finely sliced
8 anchovy fillets from a
    jar, roughly chopped
3 garlic cloves, crushed
100g pitted black olives,
    roughly chopped
500g lamb neck, diced
400ml dry rosé wine
400ml chicken stock
1 rosemary sprig
Fine sea salt and coarsely
    ground black pepper

To make the sauce, heat a large saucepan or casserole over a high heat and, once hot, add the butter and oil. Add the onion and anchovy fillets and fry, stirring, until the onion starts to soften and colour slightly. Add the garlic, olives and lamb, stir to coat, then add the wine, stock and rosemary. Bring to the boil, reduce to a simmer and cook, partially covered, for 2–3 hours until the lamb is tender and the sauce has reduced. Give it a stir every now and again. Once the sauce is cooked, taste it before adding any salt or even pepper. I found mine to be already strong enough, thanks to the slow reduction.

When the sauce is ready, cook the pasta according to the packet instructions, but ensure the water is very well salted. Reserve 100ml of the pasta cooking water, then drain the pasta well. Mix the pasta into the sauce, along with the olive oil, reserved pasta cooking water and parsley before serving.

Real Ragu with Tagliatelle

The British staple of spaghetti Bolognese couldn't be further from the dish's true original identity. First, ragu Bolognese is definitely not served with spaghetti – the feeble strands of pasta just can't cling onto that thick slick of sauce. Most important, the sauce is a meat sauce, not a tomato sauce; so using canned tomatoes is an absolute no. I really hate to be so strict about food (especially seeing as I have deviated a little here by using mixed spice) but when you try this version I think your understanding of 'spag bol' will be recalibrated for the better. And, as with the Lamb and Black Olives recipe (page 150), don't forget to reserve the pasta cooking water to let the sauce down a little – that's the key to achieving a sauce that is rich, but not overpowering.

Heat the oil and butter in a large saucepan or casserole over a medium heat. When the butter has melted, add the pancetta and cook, stirring occasionally, until the fat renders down and the pancetta is only just slightly crispy. Add the onion, carrots and celery, stir to coat in all the fat, then cook very slowly until soft – a good 20 minutes at the very least – stirring every so often.

Once the vegetables are soft, increase the heat to high and stir in the tomato purée and mixed spice just for a minute or two, then add the wine, milk and herbs. Add the chopped brisket, bring to the boil, reduce to a very low simmer and cook, partially covered with a lid, for 3 hours. Give the pan a stir every so often to ensure the bottom isn't catching, but apart from that, sit back and soak up all of the gorgeous smell as the ragu slowly cooks.

When the ragu is ready – it will be thick and the meat will be oh so tender – season to taste. Cook the pasta according to the packet instructions, but ensure the water is very well salted. Reserve 100ml of the pasta cooking water, then drain. Add the pasta to the ragu pan along with the reserved pasta water, the olive oil and parsley. Stir well to mix. Serve with a scattering of Parmesan.

SERVES 4

For the ragu sauce

2 tbsp olive oil

50g unsalted butter

200g smoked pancetta, finely chopped

1 onion, finely chopped

2 carrots, finely chopped

2 celery sticks, finely chopped

3 tbsp tomato purée

1 tbsp ground mixed spice

500ml red wine

500ml milk

2 dried bay leaves

2 rosemary sprigs

Fine sea salt and coarsely ground black pepper

1kg beef brisket, in 1cm dice

To serve

500g dried tagliatelle pasta

75ml extra virgin olive oil (I prefer Ligurian)

Small handful of parsley, roughly chopped

100g Parmesan, finely grated

Duck Leg Confit with Celeriac Mash & Balsamic Red Cabbage

The first time I had confit de canard was on a college trip to Montpellier. I sat with my teachers, Odile and Flo, who were just the coolest gals. The air was sweet as my friends and I ate, drank red wine and chatted for hours. I'd never tasted duck prepared like this before: so tender and melting. You need to start preparing the confit a day before you want to serve it, but it's so worth it. I dedicate this recipe to Odile and Flo, with thanks for their inspiration and guidance.

SERVES 2

For the duck confit
3 tbsp sea salt flakes
2 dried bay leaves
2 large duck legs
800g duck or
  goose fat

**For the balsamic
red cabbage**
¼ red cabbage,
  very finely shredded
½ tsp sea salt flakes
1 tbsp balsamic
  vinegar

For the mash
400g celeriac, diced
400g King Edward
  potatoes, diced
  smaller than
  the celeriac
1 tbsp soured cream
Fine sea salt

The day before you want to cook everything, prepare the duck. Scatter half the salt flakes into a roasting tray and add the bay leaves. Place the duck legs on top, scattering the rest of the salt over them. Cover the tray with clingfilm and place into the fridge for 12 hours.

The next day, brush off the salt. Put the fat into a saucepan and set over a medium heat, allowing the fat to melt completely. Once it has melted, add the duck legs, ensuring they are completely submerged, and set over a low-medium heat. Cook the duck for 2–2½ hours, until the meat is so tender that it is almost falling off the bone. You don't have to finish the duck now – submerge it entirely in the fat, let the fat set, and it will keep in the fridge for weeks on end.

On the day you wish to serve the duck, put the cabbage, salt and vinegar into a bowl and leave to macerate for 30 minutes or so. The vinegar and salt will draw out the excess moisture from the cabbage, making it limp yet crunchy.

Remove the duck from the fat, scraping off as much fat as you can. Don't throw away the fat – it'll make the best roast potatoes.

Preheat the oven to 220°C/200°C fan/gas mark 7. Set an ovenproof frying pan over a high heat and add the duck, skin-side down. Fry for a few minutes to start it sizzling, then roast in the oven for 35–40 minutes until deeply golden. Flip over the legs after about 20 minutes.

Meanwhile, put the celeriac and potatoes into a large pan and cover with water. Add a generous pinch of salt and bring to the boil. Cook until the potatoes are soft. I like the celeriac to retain some texture, to make the mash a little more rustic. Drain the veg, return them to the pan and set over a high heat, stirring the pan for a minute or two to dry out everything.

Remove the pan from the heat, add the soured cream and a heaped teaspoon of the cooking fat, and mash. Season to taste – potatoes need a decent amount of salt, but add it gradually, tasting after each addition.

Serve the duck legs on top of the mash, accompanied by the macerated cabbage.

Eating In, Eking Out: One Ham Hock, Two Meals

There is little more virtuous than the eking out of an ingredient. In our age of disposable fashion and convenience food too much waste surrounds us. Leftovers so often and so sadly are discarded – a process that, for me, is almost criminal. When food is wasted, people and their energy are wasted; we were all brought up on the maxim: 'Finish your food; there are people starving.' But it travels deeper than that. To waste an ingredient shows a lack of respect for many in the food chain: the farmer who plants the vegetables or rears the animal; the worker who harvests or slaughters; the process and resources taken to package, transport and stock the produce. And our mothers were right: it is, indeed, a lack of respect for those who have nothing. Saving a plate of food won't end starvation or poverty, but it is a symbol of respect for food.

This recipe is a great way to cook simply and have enough for two meals.

Shredded Ham Hock

1 ham hock,
  weighing 1–1.3kg
1 carrot, quartered
1 fennel bulb,
  quartered
1 unpeeled onion,
  quartered

Put the ham hock into a pot with the vegetables. Cover with water and bring to the boil, then reduce to a simmer, cover with a lid and cook for 2 hours or until the meat is tender. Remove the hock from the water, allow to cool, then shred into small chunks.

Sauerkraut & Bay Ham Hock Skillet

A skillet, also known as a hash, is an American dish of fried deliciousness. The name comes from the cast-iron pan in which it is made, but any frying pan does the trick.

SERVES 2

50g unsalted butter
500g Maris Piper
   potatoes, cut
   into 1cm cubes
6 dried bay leaves
1 garlic clove,
   peeled and halved
1 tsp coarsely ground
   black pepper
1 onion,
   roughly chopped
250ml chicken stock
200g cooked ham
   hock (see left),
   shredded
150g frozen peas,
   defrosted
2 tbsp sauerkraut
Sea salt flakes

Put the butter into a large sauté or deep-sided frying pan and set over a medium heat. Once the butter has melted, add the potatoes, bay, garlic and pepper, and fry, tossing the pan every once in a while, until the potatoes are golden brown and cooked through – at least 20 minutes. Once the potatoes are cooked, increase the heat to high, add the onion and then the stock. Boil rapidly to evaporate the liquid. When the stock has almost entirely evaporated, reduce the heat to medium, add the ham hock and peas and stir through. Fry until everything is a little crispy on the base. Sprinkle over the sauerkraut and a pinch of salt and serve.

Ham Hock & Smoked Cheddar Grilled Sandwich

Pork, smoked cheese and mustard make for a punchy grilled cheese sandwich. The sweet onions and the pickled cucumbers are important here to cut through those strong flavours. The key to making a crispy grilled cheese sandwich is patience – a more gentle, longer fry is imperative.

First caramelise the onion. Heat 25g of the butter in a small saucepan over a high heat. Once the butter melts and starts to sizzle, add the onion and fry, stirring, for about 10 minutes until the onion is very soft and brown. Stir in the vinegar and sugar, then remove from the heat.

Butter the slices of bread and spread with Dijon mustard. Arrange the sliced pickled cucumbers across 2 slices of the bread and top with the ham and caramelised onions. Top that with the grated cheese, then put the top slices of bread onto the sandwiches and press down to compact.

Heat the remaining butter in a frying pan over a medium heat. Once the butter melts, add the sandwiches and fry gently until golden brown, then flip over and fry the other side – make sure you fry the sandwiches long enough for the cheese to melt.

Combine the ingredients for the mayonnaise and put into a small bowl. Serve, dipping the sandwich into the mayo before each bite.

MAKES 2

/5g salted butter,
   at room temperature
1 onion, thinly sliced
1 tsp balsamic vinegar
1 tsp caster sugar
4 thickly cut slices
   of bread
Dijon mustard
2 pickled cucumbers,
   finely sliced
150g cooked ham
   hock (see page
   156), shredded
150g smoked
   Cheddar, grated

For the mayonnaise
4 tbsp mayonnaise
2 tbsp fresh dill fronds,
   finely chopped
1 tbsp capers,
   roughly chopped
1 tbsp Dijon mustard

Schezuan & Leek Pulled Pork with Salt Roasted Pineapple

This is a special spin on the classic combination of pork, pineapple and fried egg. Szechuan peppercorns can leave your mouth feeling as though you've licked the terminals on a battery, but the slow-cooking process elevates their charming spice without the mouth-numbing quality. The pineapple salt crust helps to draw out any excess water from the fruit, leaving an intense pineapple flavour.

SERVES 4

For the pork

1kg pork shoulder, off the bone and in one piece

400g leeks, chopped into 2cm pieces

2 tbsp Szechuan peppercorns

1 litre chicken stock

For the pineapple

1 small super-sweet pineapple

400g sea salt flakes

2 large egg whites

To serve

2 tbsp sesame oil

4 large eggs

Preheat the oven to 160°C/140°C fan/gas mark 3.

Put the ingredients for the pork into a large ovenproof saucepan or casserole and bring to the boil, then reduce to simmer.

While the pan simmers, cut the bottom off the pineapple so it stands upright, then use a sharp knife to shave off the crocodile-like skin. Mix together the sea salt and egg whites in a bowl to form a paste the consistency of wet sand. Press the salt mixture onto the flesh of the pineapple – it may crumble off here and there, but try to compact it as best you can and it should stick. Put the pineapple on a small ovenproof plate or tray. Transfer the pork and pineapple into the oven and cook for 3–3½ hours, until the pork is starting to flake apart and the pineapple's salt crust has become very dry.

When you're ready to serve, heat the sesame oil in a frying pan over a medium-high heat. Once the oil is hot, add the eggs and fry gently until the white is set and the yolk is still runny – spooning the hot oil over the top of the egg as it cooks helps to speed things along. Serve shreds of pork with slices of pineapple, accompanied with the soft, sweet leeks and fried eggs.

Lamb Meatballs with Sherry & Currants

If meatballs aren't tender and melt-in-the-mouth, they're not good meatballs. These are incredibly tender, thanks to the milk, which soothes away the lamb's stubbornness. The combination here is of Moorish origin, and is oh so moreish: slightly sour, a little sweet and packed with flavour.

SERVES 2–4

For the meatballs
500g lamb mince
  (minimum 20% fat)
Ful fat milk, to cover
½ tsp bicarbonate
  of soda
2 tbsp plain flour
Sea salt flakes and
  coarsely ground
  black pepper

For the soaked currants
100g currants
150ml Oloroso sherry

For the sauce
Olive oil, for frying
1 large red onion,
  finely chopped
2 garlic cloves, minced
1 tsp cumin seeds
1 tsp ground coriander
¼ tsp ground cloves
150ml Oloroso sherry
1 tbsp tomato purée
500ml chicken stock

To serve
175g bulgar wheat
2 tbsp pine nuts
Handful of flat-leaf
  parsley, chopped

For the meatballs, put the lamb mince into a mixing bowl and cover with milk. Allow to rest for 15 minutes, but no longer than 30 minutes or the meat will become tough.

Put the currants and sherry into a small saucepan and bring to the boil. Boil for 3 minutes, until the currants are plump and juicy. Remove from the heat and set aside until needed.

Put the mince into a sieve and allow the milk to drain off. You might need to give it a squeeze to get rid of most of the milk. The meat will have become very paste-like by now and that's precisely what you want – don't be panicking. Return the mince to the bowl and add the bicarbonate of soda, flour, and a generous pinch of salt and pepper. Mix well together– I use my hands – then divide into 12–14 fairly large meatballs. Don't worry if these are more like patties than balls; this is a very soft mix, but the result will be so tender. Place on a tray and set aside.

For the sauce, heat a generous glug of oil in a large frying pan over a medium-high heat. Once the oil is hot, add the onion and fry, stirring very frequently, until soft and slightly browned. Add the garlic and spices and fry, stirring, for a minute. Pour in the sherry and allow it to bubble until evaporated, then stir in the tomato purée and fry, stirring, until brown. Stir in the soaked currants, chicken stock and a generous pinch of salt and pepper, bring to the boil, then reduce to a simmer and cover with a lid. Cook for 10 minutes, remove from the heat and set aside.

Heat another glug of oil in a deep-sided frying pan or sauté pan over a medium-high heat. Add the meatballs and fry for a few minutes on each side until browned. Add the sauce. Bring to the boil, reduce to a simmer and cook, uncovered, for 20 minutes.

Meanwhile, put the bulgar wheat into a mixing bowl and pour over boiling water, covering the wheat by 2cm. Cover with clingfilm, and leave for 15 minutes until tender. After this time, drain away any excess water and season with a pinch of salt and pepper.

Heat a frying pan over a high heat and add the pine nuts. Toss for a minute or so until their aroma is strong and they've taken on a little colour. Stir through the bulgar wheat with the parsley and serve with the meatballs.

Guinness & Blackberry Beef Stew

Beef slow-cooked in beer is no novelty. What makes this stew a new star is the fruit. Blackberries are easily manipulated. Dotted into a frangipane tart or boiled down with a little sugar, you'd believe their destiny was a sweet one. But they offer a savouriness too, especially when not eaten straight off the bush; their sweetness starts to ferment and sour. That confused, tart sweetness is brilliant in stews and sauces – it balances the other flavours. A note on the relish: don't omit it.

Preheat the oven to 160°C/140°C fan/gas mark 3.

Put the steak into a mixing bowl and add the flour and a generous pinch of salt and pepper. Toss together – I use my hands – until the beef is evenly coated. Heat a generous glug of oil in a large ovenproof casserole or saucepan. Once the oil is hot (it will shimmer gently), add the beef and fry, turning once, until coloured. You'll need to do this in at least two batches; if you overcrowd the pan, the meat will braise rather than fry and you won't achieve the colour or depth of flavour.

Once all of the meat has been fried, return it to the pan with the remaining ingredients. Bring to the boil, then cover with a lid and cook in the oven for 2–3 hours, until the meat is tender and flaking.

To make the relish, simply combine the ingredients in a bowl and allow to sit at room temperature until needed. Serve the stew with some of the relish over it.

SERVES 4

1kg braising steak, diced
2 tbsp plain flour
Sunflower or olive
  oil, for frying
440ml can Guinness
250ml beef stock
1 red onion,
  roughly chopped
3 parsnips, diced
3 carrots, diced
200g blackberries
3 dried bay leaves
Sea salt flakes and
  coarsely ground
  black pepper

For the relish
1 red onion, finely sliced
200g blackberries, halved
5 tbsp red wine vinegar
1 tbsp caster sugar

Eating In, Eking Out: Salt Beef

Although I am devoted to my craft, I'm immensely impatient, and so the prospect of waiting a week for a particular meal is a little testing. But when I first made salt beef, it was a revelation: it's so simple, and it instilled in me a new-found patience for the longer processes in cookery.

The beef is brined for a week before being slowly poached. The result is a cut so tender it can be sliced and eaten with fingers and a smile. And the added beauty lies in how it is easily eked out across a few meals. I use dark muscovado sugar in this brine. It gives the beef a darker colour and perfumes it with its gentle earthiness.

During the brining process, the meat must be submerged entirely and it should be stored in a non-reactive container – I use an extra-large plastic mixing bowl that has been through a hot cycle in the dishwasher.

Muscovado Salt Beef

Put the brine ingredients in a large saucepan or casserole and bring to the boil. Boil for 1 minute, then turn off the heat and allow the solution to cool to room temperature.

If the brisket has been rolled and stringed, remove the string and unroll it – this will allow the brine to work deeper into the meat. Once the brine has cooled to room temperature, put the brisket into your vessel of choice and pour the solution over it, or enough to completely submerge the meat. The beef will try to float, so cover the surface of the brine with clingfilm, and place a heavy object on top – if you're using a large plastic bowl as I do, just pop a plate and a can of beans on top and that ensures the meat is submerged fully. Leave in a cool place – fridge or cold room – for a week.

After the week, remove the beef from the brine and rinse it under cold water. Put it into a large saucepan or casserole with the celery, onions, garlic and peppercorns and cover with water. Bring to the boil, then reduce the heat so that the water is steaming with the occasional bubble, but don't let it simmer quickly. Cook for 3–4 hours, until the beef is tender. You might need to add a little more hot water from the kettle every now and again, if the water evaporates.

If you are eating the salt beef freshly cooked (I recommend serving with boiled, buttered new potatoes, hot mustard and nothing more, or make the bagels on page 120), let it rest for 30 minutes before serving. Otherwise, let the beef cool, then wrap in clingfilm and refrigerate.

2.5kg beef brisket
2 celery sticks,
    roughly chopped
2 onions, unpeeled
    and quartered
1 garlic bulb, halved
1 tbsp green peppercorns

For the brine
2.5 litres cold water
275g dark muscovado sugar
350g salt (fine or flaked
    sea salt, not rock salt)
1 tbsp green peppercorns
½ tbsp juniper berries
5 cloves
8 bay leaves

Salt Beef, Wilted Rocket & Lancashire Cheese Pide

Pide, Turkish flatbread, comes in as many forms and variations as its Italian cousin pizza. Wilted spinach and spices are a common topping, but instead I like to use rocket, which has a fresher, more peppery bite. These little bread boats are the perfect vessels to carry my succulent salt beef from plate to mouth.

To make the dough, put the flour, salt and yeast into a bowl and add the milk. Bring the mixture together with your hands to form a stiff dough, then knead until the dough is smooth – about 10 minutes by hand, quicker in a KitchenAid food processor fitted with a dough hook. Put the dough into a lightly oiled bowl, cover with clingfilm, and allow the dough to rest until doubled in size – because this is a fairly stiff dough, it will take that bit longer.

Meanwhile prepare the topping. Heat the oil in a frying pan set over a high heat and add the onion. As the onion sizzles, reduce the heat to medium-high and cook, stirring frequently, for 10 minutes or until the onion is soft and ever so slightly coloured. Add the cumin to the pan and fry for a further minute, then add the rocket and stir through until it wilts down completely. Remove the pan from the heat and add the sumac, beef and parsley, along with a generous pinch of salt.

Preheat the oven to 240°C/220°C fan/gas mark 9 and place a pizza stone or baking sheet in the oven to get hot.

When the dough has doubled in size, divide it into four equal portions. Dust the worktop liberally with flour and roll out each portion into a fairly thin oblong. Pile the topping down the centre of each oblong, leaving a 2cm margin around the edge of the dough. Fold the long edges up over the filling, and then twist the shorter edges to form the classic boat shape. Place the pides onto a well-floured baking sheet, crumble over the cheese and then slide the pides off the baking sheet and onto the hot pizza stone or sheet in the oven. Bake for 5–7 minutes, until the dough is brown and the cheese has melted. Drizzle over a little olive oil – extra virgin if you have it to hand – and serve.

MAKES 4

For the dough

300g strong white
　　bread flour, plus
　　extra for dusting
5g fine sea salt
7g sachet fast-action yeast
175ml warm milk
Olive oil

For the topping

1 tbsp olive oil
1 onion, finely chopped
1 tsp ground cumin
75g rocket, washed
1 tsp ground sumac
200g cooked salt beef,
　　shredded (see page 167)
20g flat-leaf parsley,
　　roughly chopped
100g Creamy Lancashire
　　cheese, crumbled
Sea salt flakes

Salt Beef Hash

Corned beef hash is in my blood. My mini mum Irene (my mother-in-law) makes the best version – a dish to which nothing will ever compare for my partner. While I don't wish to alter something so heavily entrenched in British culinary history, made with salt beef this is very special. If you're using a good-quality beef stock with bags of flavour, there's no need for Worcestershire sauce, but if you like that, feel free. I always eat this, as any Lancashire lad would, with thickly buttered white bread. The real point of contention, one that has divided families for years, is: ketchup or brown sauce?

SERVES 4

50g unsalted butter
1 tbsp sunflower oil
4 Maris Piper potatoes,
  peeled and cubed
1 onion, thinly sliced
1 carrot, finely diced
2 celery sticks,
  finely diced
1 litre beef stock
500g cooked salt
  beef, shredded
  (see page 167)
Fine sea salt and
  coarsely ground
  black pepper

Heat the butter and oil in a large saucepan or casserole over a medium-high heat, add the potatoes, onion, carrot and celery and fry for 10 minutes. Increase the heat to high, add the stock and bring to the boil. Reduce to a simmer and cook, uncovered, for 30 minutes. Add the shredded salt beef and cook for a further 15 minutes until the stew is thick and the potatoes have started to break down. Test for seasoning and serve in bowls with your sauce of choice.

Use any leftover hash in the recipe overleaf.

Eking Further: Salt Beef Hash Eggs Benedict

During a snowstorm in Banff, Canada, we took refuge at Storm Mountain Lodge. It might have been the cosiest place on earth. The snow outside was deep and endless, while we stayed inside by the crackling fire. We ate salt beef with eggs Benedict and listened to folk music. While the weather here in Lancashire is poor, and my log-burning stove is cosy, nothing quite compares to the intense chill and cosiness we felt in Canada. This Lancashire version of that meal, however, is miles better.

For the Hollandaise sauce, set a heatproof bowl over a pan of barely simmering water and add the egg yolks, vinegar and mustard. Whisk to combine. Ensure the melted butter is still very hot and slowly add it, drop by drop, whisking well after each addition – if you add the butter too quickly, the sauce will be sure to split. After you've added the first quarter of the butter, you can pour the butter into the bowl in a very thin stream while you whisk constantly. Once you have a smooth, thick, buttery sauce, remove the pan from the heat, leaving the bowl of Hollandaise above the water to keep warm. Whisk in lemon juice and salt, to taste.

Slice the muffin in half and toast. To poach the eggs, bring a deep-sided frying pan of water to the boil and then turn the heat to the lowest setting. Don't bother to stir the water or add vinegar; just crack the eggs onto a plate (one at a time) and gently slide each egg into the water. Allow the eggs to cook for a few minutes until the white is firm, but the yolk is still soft.

Top each muffin half with the salt beef hash, then place a poached egg on top and finish with the Hollandaise and a splatter of Tabasco sauce.

SERVES 2

For the
Hollandaise sauce
2 large egg yolks
1 tbsp white wine vinegar
1 tsp English mustard
150g unsalted
   butter, melted
Squeeze of lemon juice
Fine sea salt

To serve
1 English muffin
2 very fresh large eggs
150g leftover
   Salt Beef Hash
   (see page 170), heated
Tabasco sauce

something sweet

Sweet Belonging

I don't think it possible to deny the inherent femininity of baking. Plenty of men have carved careers in desserts, putting their masculine marks on mousses, serving towering afternoon teas of testosterone. But the provenance of it all, for me, lies in the tenderness of the women in my life.

The clichéd memories I have of my mother in her apron, standing gracefully stirring pots and pans, preparing the tea for her children and husband, are mere snippets in time. That soft femininity is what I loved most about seeing my mother cook, but merely hours before that, she'd woken at 4am to milk cows and battle with bulls in the field. She organised a crew of unruly, all-male, farm hands, at the same time as project-managing a building renovation. That moment in time as the perfect housewife was merely the soft centre of a woman made of titanium.

It is that softness that guides me when I bake. As I make cakes or puddings I am reminded of mum hollowing channels of tenderness into great mountains of flour, and breathing air into folds of cloudy whipped cream. Baking is an occupation that must be entered into and undertaken with nothing but love in the heart, or the results will be disappointing and soulless.

I believe the cravings we have for something sweet stem from wanting to feel safe. From the moment we are born we latch onto our mothers to draw that sweet, life-giving elixir. Even if we are raised on a manmade alternative to breast milk, it is still delivered with proximity and tenderness. That's where it stems from. We learn to associate sweet with comfort. Baking, like eating comfort food, is a process whereby familiarity is regained.

Cynics may tell you that this chapter and its contents are all about sugar, how sugar is a beast that fuels addiction. That would be a reductive point of view. This transcends sugar; this is about belonging. I don't bake so I can gorge on 16 brownies – sometimes I won't even have one. I bake to reattach myself to my family, to feel like I belong. There is a difference between stuffing as many bars of chocolate into your mouth as possible and enjoying a slice of homemade cake. A slice of cake contains plenty of 'bad' ingredients (mind you, this whole book does, and if you're still reading, then you're already on board and perhaps I needn't harp on), but a slice of cake every so often and two glasses of whisky a night didn't do my great grandma too much harm: she died aged 93. A slice of cake after a lunch packed with vegetables is, for me, a much more balanced idea of diet than a regime centred on reduced carbohydrate intake.

Apple Cider Crullers

These aren't at all dissimilar to the Spanish doughnut treat, churros. In fact, they're pretty much the same thing, only shaped in rings rather than fat, spikey sausages. The pastry itself is just a choux pastry, which isn't at all difficult – although it mistakenly has the reputation of being tricky to make. It isn't. To amp up the flavour I use a dry cider in place of water, which gives the pastry that apple undertone.

For the choux pastry, put the cider, salt and butter into a small saucepan and set over a low heat just until the butter melts, then increase the heat to high. Once the liquid starts to boil, remove from the heat and quickly stir in the flour with a wooden spoon – you must do this vigorously and quickly to form a very thick, smooth dough. Put the pan back on the heat, stirring to dry out and smooth the dough – about a minute. Put the dough into a mixer fitted with a paddle attachment. Beat the eggs in a bowl and add, a drop at a time, to the cooled dough, beating very well after each addition until it is completely incorporated. You may not need all of the egg; once the mixture is smooth and falls reluctantly from the spatula to form a V-shape, it's ready. Put the choux into the piping bag fitted with a large star nozzle.

Pipe the pastry into 7cm-diameter rings on the squares of baking paper.

Preheat the deep-fat fryer to 175°C. Place the pieces of baking paper, cruller-side down, into the oil, then remove the baking paper with kitchen tongs. Fry for a minute or two per side until golden brown and crispy. Remove with a slotted spoon and set onto kitchen paper to blot off the excess oil.

For the glaze, sift the icing sugar, then whisk in enough cider to make a thick icing. Dip the crullers into the icing and then dust with cinnamon and serve.

MAKES ABOUT 12

For the choux pastry
125ml dry apple cider
1/8 tsp fine sea salt
50g unsalted butter, cubed
85g strong white bread flour
2 large eggs

For the glaze
250g icing sugar
3 tbsp apple cider
Cinnamon, for dusting

Equipment
Piping bag fitted with a large star nozzle
12 x 8cm squares of baking paper
Deep-fat fryer with clean, unscented vegetable oil

Ultimate Apple Pie

The magic of a perfect apple pie lies in the cooking down of the apples – so many apple pies or crumbles disappoint. On the one hand you have the undercooked: lumps of crunchy apple floating around in a too-watery, insipid juice. On the other there is the overcooked: sloppy apple purée that even a rapacious toothless babe would decline. Apples need proper attention. Here, the first half is cooked down until very soft before the second half is added and cooked just until tender. This method ensures a thick filling, but one with texture.

For the pastry, put the flour, sugar and salt into a bowl and toss together. Rub the butter into the dry ingredients until you have a breadcrumb-like consistency. Add the water, a tablespoon at a time, until the mixture comes together into a smooth dough. (It's much easier to just throw the dry ingredients into a food processor, blend in the butter, then slowly add the water until the pastry clumps together.) Turn out onto a lightly floured surface and knead briefly by hand (no more than 30 seconds – just until smooth), then flatten into a disc and wrap in clingfilm. Chill for 30 minutes.

Meanwhile make the filling. Peel and core the apples and chop them into roughly 1cm chunks and put into a bowl with the lemon juice.

Heat a large sauté pan or saucepan over a high heat and add the sugar, butter and half of the apple chunks. Bring to the boil, then reduce to a quick simmer and cook for 25 minutes or so, until when you gently squeeze a chunk of apple it is soft and spongy. Keep an eye on the pan and give it a stir every so often. Once the apples have cooked down, add the remaining apples, bring back to the boil, reduce to a quick simmer again and cook until they are spongy; the first lot of apples will have turned mushy by now. Stir in the calvados and vanilla and allow to cool.

Preheat the oven to 200°C/180°C fan/gas mark 6.

Roll out three-quarters of the pastry and use it to line a 23cm pie tin, trimming off the excess pastry. Pile the filling into the pastry case. Roll out the remaining pastry and cut out 10 strips about 3cm wide and long enough to form a lattice over the top of the pie. Arrange the strips over the pie and trim off the excess pastry. Glaze the pastry with the beaten egg and bake for 45 minutes. Serve warm or cold.

Variation
If you're partial to the sweet almond taste of marzipan, it works well in the pie. Substitute the calvados with amaretto, and after the filling has cooled grate 100g marzipan into it.

SERVES 8

For the pastry
400g plain flour, plus
   extra for dusting
1 tbsp caster sugar
1 tsp fine sea salt
200g unsalted butter,
   at room temperature
8–10 tbsp cold water
1 egg, beaten, to glaze

For the filling
6 Granny Smith apples
6 Braeburn apples
Juice of 1 lemon
170g light brown
   muscovado sugar
75g unsalted butter
1 tbsp calvados
   or brandy
1 tbsp vanilla bean paste

Goat's Cheese, Rhubarb & Thyme Cheesecake

You might take one look at this title, purse your lips, then slam my book shut, but just wait (if you've made it this far, you know your subconscious is intrigued). This is superb – perhaps the best cheesecake I've ever made, or indeed, eaten. The goat's cheese is added to help tart the cheesecake up, in both title and flavour; it doesn't taste exclusively of that, but it has a certain sour quality that isn't achievable with just cream cheese. Thyme is such an adaptable herb, anyway, that it just echoes through this dessert without overpowering anything. If rhubarb is unavailable, just stew down some sharp blackberries or gooseberries with a little sugar.

SERVES 8–10

For the base
250g digestive biscuits
50g Ryvita
80g unsalted butter

For the filling
300g soft goat's cheese
  (I like Rosary)
600g full-fat
  cream cheese
100ml buttermilk
1 tbsp cornflour
150g caster sugar
3 large eggs

For the topping
200g rhubarb,
  roughly chopped
175g caster sugar
4 thyme sprigs

Preheat the oven to 200°C/180°C fan/gas mark 6. Grease a 20cm square cake tin and line the base with baking paper.

For the base, put the biscuits and Ryvita into a food processor and pulse to a fine crumb. Add the butter and blend until you have a damp sandy consistency. Tip the mixture into the cake tin and compress to the bottom with your hands or the back of a spoon, then bake for 15 minutes to set. Remove the tin from the oven and allow to cool, though do leave the oven on.

For the filling, whisk the goat's cheese, cream cheese and buttermilk with the cornflour, until well combined – I do this in my KitchenAid fitted with the whisk attachment, but an electric hand-held beater would work fine. Add the sugar and whisk just until incorporated, then beat in the eggs until you have a smooth, fairly runny batter. Pour the cheesecake batter on top of the base and put it into the oven. Immediately reduce the heat of the oven to 140°C/120°C fan/gas mark 1. Bake for 1 hour – 1 hour 10 minutes, until the cheesecake is set but has quite an impressive wobble to it when gently shaken.

Allow the cheesecake to cool to room temperature and then refrigerate overnight (I know it's quite a wait, but it needs that length of time to set; though a few hours would be okay if you're really in urgent need of cheesecake).

For the topping, put the rhubarb and sugar into a saucepan over a medium-high heat with a splash of water and the thyme. Bring to the boil and cook until the rhubarb has given up entirely and you have a very loose jam. Pluck the thyme stalks out while you can, then leave to cool to room temperature. To serve, either pour the rhubarb mixture over the entire cheesecake and reveal in full grandeur, or serve slices with a little of the rhubarb mixture blobbed on top.

Fig, Prune & Port Tarte Tatin

I'd make a lousy criminal: I'm just too honest. My family say of me, 'He cannot hold his own water.' And so, I admit, your honour, that this was an idea I stole from the great Nigel Slater. And I did so without guilt; we are standing on the shoulders of giants, after all. But one thing I would never do is copy a recipe and pass it off as my own. This tart is based on one of Nigel's – his dried fig and marsala tart – but the marriage of fig, prune and port is one I've loved for ages; it's a combination I use with spices in place of mincemeat in my Christmas mince pies.

Put the figs and prunes into a bowl and pour over the port. Leave for as long as you can bear – an hour would just about do it, but overnight would be better. Once the fruit is soaked, only then can you continue.

Preheat the oven to 200°C/180°C fan/gas mark 6.

Flour the work surface and roll out the pastry until fairly thin – around 5mm ideally. Using an upturned ovenproof frying pan as a guide (mine's 23cm at the base), cut out a disc of pastry that is slightly bigger in diameter than that of the pan. Repeatedly stab the pastry with a fork to help it rise evenly. Put the pastry in the fridge until needed.

Place the frying pan over a medium-heat and, once it's hot, add the sugar. Allow the sugar to melt and turn a deep golden caramel colour. Add the butter and swirl the pan to deglaze, then add the soaked fruit, port and all. Place the pastry disc on top and tuck the surplus down into the pan – if you value your fingertips, you'll use a wooden spoon.

Pop the tart into the oven and bake for 25–30 minutes, until the pastry is puffed up, golden brown and very crispy. Remove from the oven and invert immediately onto a large plate – it's wise to cover your arms with a tea towel, or wear a thick jumper; sugar burns are particularly painful. Enjoy warm.

SERVES 8–10

500g dried figs,
  left whole
200g dried prunes,
  left whole
150ml ruby port
Flour, for dusting
300g all-butter
  puff pastry
150g caster sugar
40g unsalted butter

Clementine & Cardamom Upside-down Cake

Most families have a favourite upside-down cake, a staple of British home comfort. I was tempted to rekindle my love of the pineapple version, but that was skating too close to the cheesy retro style for my liking. And I don't think it pertinent to 'pimp' canned pineapple and cake. This is a refreshing version; perhaps surprisingly, clementines turn fairly sour when cooked this way, which is lovely against the bittersweet caramel. Cardamom is a ghostly spice, haunting right to the very soul of this cake.

SERVES 10–12

For the topping
125g caster sugar
8 clementines

For the cake
285g unsalted butter
285g light brown
  muscovado sugar
5 large eggs, beaten
285g self-raising flour
1½ tsp ground
  cardamom
1 tsp fine sea salt

For the glaze
(optional)
4 tbsp apricot jam
1 tbsp water

Preheat the oven to 170°C/150°C fan/gas mark 3. Grease a 23cm round loose-bottomed cake tin and line with baking paper.

For the topping, heat a medium saucepan over a medium-high heat. Once the pan is hot, add the sugar and allow it to melt and slowly turn to an amber caramel – the sugar touching the base of the pan will turn first, and slowly but surely the sugar on top will soon become liquid, too. Give the pan a little swirl as the sugar starts to melt. Once you have a dark caramel, pour it into the base of the prepared cake tin.

Keeping them whole, peel the clementines, then cut them in half horizontally to retain that little hole in the top and bottom. Arrange the clementine halves, hump-side down, on the caramel.

For the cake, cream together the butter and sugar until really soft – the butter should become very pale and the sugar will more or less dissolve into it. Add the eggs, a little at a time, beating well after each addition, then add the flour, cardamom and salt and beat in just until incorporated to a smooth batter. I do all of this in my KitchenAid fitted with the paddle attachment, but an electric hand-held mixer will do. Pour the batter over the clementines and gently level it out, being careful not to displace the fruits. Bake for 1 hour and up to 1 hour 10 minutes, until a skewer inserted into the centre of the cake comes out clean, apart from the odd crumb of cake made soggy by the oranges beneath. Remove the cake from the oven and allow it to cool in the tin for 5 minutes, then invert onto a plate.

For the glaze, simply combine the jam and water in a small pan and bring to the boil. Paint the glaze onto the cake with a pastry brush. The cake will keep for a few days in an airtight tin; it'll actually be that bit better on day two.

Ovaltine Banana Malt Loaf

At bedtime on a Sunday evening, just after 'You've Been Framed' had ended on the TV, I would feign sleepiness to avoid climbing the stairs. After a while, my parents latched on to my plan and would play me at my own game: 'If he was really asleep, he'd have one arm up in the air.' An arm would slowly unfurl from the comfy depths of the sofa. 'But if he was completely asleep, he'd say, "Ovaltine".' I'd mumble the word twice through lazy lips. Compelled by my cuteness, they'd still carry me off to bed. I don't drink Ovaltine these days, but whenever I get a waft of its super-sweet malt, I'm always reminded of those bedtime games.

If the bananas aren't ripe yet, there's no need to wait a week until they blacken. Simply pop them, in their skins, onto a roasting tray and bake in a hot oven for about 15 minutes until they blacken. Allow them to cool before using.

This isn't light and airy like a banana bread, but is dense, fudgy and malty, like the bought malt loaf I used to enjoy – and indeed still do – slathered with salty butter.

Preheat the oven to 180°C/160°C fan/gas mark 4. Grease a 900g loaf tin and line with baking paper.

Mash the bananas to a purée – I just use a fork. Sift the flour, Ovaltine and baking powder into a mixing bowl and add the sugars. Stir together to combine well. Combine the eggs, oil and banana purée in a jug. Pour the wet ingredients into the dry ingredients and fold until you have a smooth batter. Scoop the batter into the prepared loaf tin and level out the surface. Bake for 45–60 minutes, or until a skewer inserted into the loaf comes out relatively clean, apart from, perhaps, a smear of banana. Allow to cool in the tin.

For the frosting, beat together the butter and icing sugar until pale and fluffy, then add the cream cheese and beat in until smooth. I tend to do this in a mixing bowl with a hand-held electric beater, as I find my KitchenAid to be a little too ferocious, splitting the cream cheese.

Once the loaf has cooled, remove it from the tin and spread the frosting on top. Finish with a light dusting of Ovaltine.

SERVES 8–10

350g ripe bananas
  (peeled weight)
175g plain flour
60g Ovaltine
2 tsp baking powder
80g caster sugar
80g light brown
  muscovado sugar
2 large eggs
4 tbsp sunflower oil

For the frosting
100g unsalted
  butter, softened
100g icing sugar
200g full-fat
  cream cheese
1 tsp Ovaltine,
  for dusting

Cherry & Amaretti Crumble Cake

This is my version of the classic cherry and almond cake. I always use those dark cherries soaked in kirsch – their flavour is intense and boozy. When I drain the cherries I reserve the syrup to add a sweet kick to my coffees. The crumble topping adds another almond dimension in the form of crunchy amaretti and flaked nuts. This is best served with a dollop of tangy crème fraîche.

SERVES 8–10

For the cake

175g unsalted
  butter, softened
175g light brown
  muscovado sugar
1 tsp almond extract
Zest of 1 unwaxed lemon
2 large eggs
100g soured cream
175g self-raising flour
½ tsp fine sea salt

For the crumble

150g self-raising flour
100g cold unsalted
  butter, cubed
75g light brown
  muscovado sugar
75g amaretti biscuits,
  crushed
40g flaked almonds

For the cherry layer

250g (drained weight)
  cherries soaked in kirsch

Preheat the oven to 180°C/160°C fan/gas mark 4. Grease a 23cm round, loose-bottomed cake tin and line the base with baking paper.

For the cake, cream the butter, sugar, almond extract and lemon zest until lighter in texture and paler in colour. Add the eggs and soured cream and beat until smooth – don't worry if it curdles – then add the flour and salt and fold together until you have a smooth batter. Scrape the batter into the cake tin and level off.

For the crumble, rub together the flour and butter until you have a breadcrumb consistency, then toss through the sugar, biscuits and almonds.

Scatter the cherries over the cake batter, as evenly as possible, and top with the crumble topping mixture.

Bake the cake in the oven for 35–40 minutes, or until a skewer inserted comes out clean (apart from the red juice of the cherries). Leave to cool completely, then transfer from the tin to a cake stand or plate to serve.

Saffron Poached Pear & Pistachio Tortes

This is an Eastern take on the classic pear frangipane tart. The pears are first poached in saffron syrup to give them a bright golden colour and gentle flavour, and pistachios are used instead of almonds. Ground pistachios are hard to come by, so I grind my own – just use a coffee grinder or one of those bullet things intended for juicing.

First poach the pears. Put the sugar, water and saffron into a saucepan and bring to the boil. Once the syrup is boiling, reduce to a brisk simmer and drop in the pears. Cover the pan with a cartouche – a disc of baking paper with a small hole cut out from the centre. This will keep the pears submerged, so long as the cartouche is touching the surface of the syrup and has a little syrup on top to weigh it down. Poach the pears until they are easily pierced with a knife, but retain their shape – a good 15–20 minutes should do it.

Preheat the oven to 200°C/180°C fan/gas mark 6. Grease 4 × 9cm fluted tart tins that are 2cm deep and line the bases with baking paper.

For the pistachio torte, beat the ingredients together to a fairly smooth batter and divide between the prepared tins as evenly as possible. Cut each pear in half, trying as best you can to cut through the stalk, then fan each half – cut small slices from top to bottom, leaving a little flesh uncut at the top (the stalk end), enabling you to fan the slices open. Place each fanned pear half on top of a torte. Bake for 30–35 minutes, until dark and crusty on top.

Heat the apricot jam and water in a small pan until you have a runny glaze – if there are lumps of pulp, just pass it through a fine sieve. Glaze each torte liberally as soon as they come out of the oven, then sprinkle over some pearl sugar and chopped pistachios.

MAKES 4

For the poached pears
2 small Comice pears,
   peeled and cored,
   stalks intact
600g caster sugar
600ml water
Generous pinch of
   saffron strands

For the pistachio torte
70g ground pistachios
60g unsalted butter,
   softened
60g light brown
   muscovado sugar
1 large egg

To finish
4 tbsp apricot jam
1 tbsp water
Pearl sugar, to sprinkle
Chopped pistachios,
   to sprinkle

Decadent Porridges

Porridge is one of those foods that we easily overlook, but it is ever present, seeking to soothe us. Like a stern grandmother, its appearance is dour, but deep beneath its conservative stance lies a heart bursting with love and the need to provide shelter.

The way we prepare our porridge is deeply personal: some like it thick, almost like rubber, to chew on in hearty fashion; others prefer it silky and thin, almost like a crème anglaise punctuated by flakes of softened oat. As a child, I used to love watching my dad make his morning porridge: an egg cup of oats, four or five egg cups of milk and water. He'd microwave it, and as I'd stand staring at the clunky old machine, watching as the porridge spun and started to breathe and swell, he'd pull me away from the microwave, saying: 'Don't stand too close or you'll frazzle your brain.'

For me, he'd prepare a bowlful of porridge in a fairly shallow bowl, so it would cool down a little more quickly. He'd always pour cold milk on top, finished with a drizzle of golden syrup. 'Start eating from the edge of the bowl,' he'd instruct, 'to stop you burning your mouth.' As with porridge itself, I've always overlooked that memory until now, but in the mere preparation of that single bowlful, the house became a deep cavern, love echoing about its walls.

Porridge can be experimental, too, decadent even. I recently caught my mum, mid-scoop, piling ice cream on top of her steaming porridge. At first I grimaced, but on further consideration it makes perfect sense: hot and cold; sweet and salty; the idea was genius. It compelled me to experiment for myself, and the results are something I'm going to enjoy frequently for those lavish Sunday brunches.

Crème Brulée Porridge

SERVES 1

The Crème Brulée Porridge here embodies the essence of the classic French dessert: a custard flavour with a deeply caramelised top. Because the porridge is wetter than a set custard, the brulée top doesn't set with a crack (it would if you chilled the porridge first) but it gives that dark sugar flavour, with the most addictive chewiness.

Put the porridge oats, milk and custard powder into a saucepan and set over a high heat. Stirring constantly, allow the mixture to come to the boil, then reduce the heat to medium and cook, still stirring, to the consistency you prefer. Stir in the lemon zest, vanilla and as much sugar as you think it needs, though do bear in mind that the top will be sweet, then pour into a heatproof bowl – preferably a wide, shallow one.

For the brulée, sprinkle the demerara sugar on top of the porridge then, with a chef's blowtorch, burn the sugar until it melts and turns to a mottled, dark caramel. If you don't have a blowtorch, just preheat the grill while you make the porridge and, ensuring your porridge is in a heatproof bowl, just grill until the sugar blackens.

For the porridge
50g jumbo porridge oats
325ml full-fat milk
1 tbsp custard powder
Zest of ½ unwaxed lemon
½ tsp vanilla bean
  paste or extract
1–3 tsp caster sugar,
  to taste

For the brulée
4 tsp demerara sugar

Salted Chocolate Porridge with Caramel Ice Cream & Salted Peanuts

SERVES 1

This porridge is an ode to my mother's invention, but with a view to propel it even deeper into the realms of decadence.

Put the porridge oats and milk into a saucepan and set over a high heat. Stirring constantly, allow the mixture to come to the boil, then reduce the heat to medium and cook, still stirring, to the consistency you prefer. Remove the pan from the heat and throw in the chocolate, stirring to entice it to melt, before adding the sugar, if any, to taste, and salt.

Pour the porridge into a bowl and top with the ice cream and peanuts.

For the porridge
50g jumbo porridge oats
325ml full-fat milk
50g dark chocolate,
  finely chopped (I go
  for 55% cocoa solids)
1 tsp sugar, or more
  or less, to taste
Generous pinch of
  sea salt flakes

To finish
1 large scoop caramel
  ice cream
25g salted peanuts,
  roughly chopped

something sweet

Smoky Hot Chocolate

This is incredible: a hot chocolate that encapsulates the campfire smell in every sip. Even if you are stuck in an urban jungle, you can still revel in countryside cosiness. Making the smoke extract is a little involved, but if you fancy half an hour or so of kitchen alchemy you won't be disappointed. I like this with a tot of Laphroaig, but you can omit the whisky entirely if you prefer.

First make the smoke extract. Steep the teabags in the boiling water for 15 minutes, then remove them, squeezing out every last drop of liquid. Discard the tea bags and have the tea ready.

Heat a saucepan over a medium-high heat and, once it's hot, add the sugar. Allow the sugar to melt and turn to a dark, amber caramel – as it melts you can stir it occasionally, but overdoing it could end in a crystallised caramel. As soon as you have a caramel, add a drop of the Lapsang tea. The caramel will sputter and hiss violently, but just ignore it. Continue adding the tea, a drop at a time, until you have incorporated all of the tea. If the caramel solidifies into a lump and appears to be rattling around the tea, simply simmer the tea until the caramel has melted into it. Remove the smoke extract from the heat. This will store in a jar in the fridge for a month or so.

To make the hot chocolate, bring the milk to the boil in a saucepan, then remove from the heat and stir in the chopped chocolate. Add the smoke extract and Laphroaig (if using) to taste. Set over a low heat to keep warm.

For the Swiss meringue marshmallow, simply put the egg white, sugar and smoke extract into a bowl and set over a pan of simmering water. Whisk constantly but gently, until the egg white is runny and the sugar has dissolved, and when you feel it with a fingertip it is hot. Remove the bowl from the heat and whisk vigorously – I use a hand-held electric beater – until a very stiff and thick meringue forms.

Decant the hot chocolate into a mug and spoon the meringue on top. If you feel the need, burnish the meringue with a chef's blowtorch.

SERVES 1

For the smoke extract
2 Lapsang Souchong
   tea bags
100ml boiling water
100g caster sugar

For the hot chocolate
1 mug of full-fat milk
45g dark chocolate
   (70% cocoa solids),
   roughly chopped
1 tbsp smoke extract
1–2 tsp Laphroaig
   whisky (optional)

**For the Swiss
meringue marshmallow**
1 large egg white
50g caster sugar
1 tsp smoke extract

Brown Butter Brownies with Hazelnuts & Salted Caramel

The number of things you can throw at a brownie without masking its comforting richness is wonderful. Salted pecan brownies are a firm favourite of mine, but I think this version might just top the charts. Whatever you prefer, the most important part is chilling or freezing the baked brownie before cutting into portions – this helps it to set.

MAKES 16

For the topping

100g hazelnuts
300g caster sugar
30g salted butter
250ml double cream
Sea salt flakes

For the brownie batter

200g unsalted butter
200g dark chocolate,
  roughly chopped
265g caster sugar
150g plain flour
3 large eggs

Preheat the oven to 200°C/180°C fan/gas mark 6. Grease a 20cm square loose-bottomed cake tin and line with baking paper.

First make the topping. Put the hazelnuts into a small dry frying pan and set it over a high heat. As the pan warms up, toss the hazelnuts every so often, until they start to brown and their ghostly smell begins to haunt. Tip into a bowl to cool, then roughly chop them

Wipe out the frying pan and set it over a medium-high heat. Sprinkle the sugar into the base of the pan and allow it to melt and turn brown – if the sugar starts to brown more quickly in some areas, just give it a gentle stir. Once you have a fairly dark-amber caramel, throw in the butter and stir it vigorously, then add the cream, a drop at a time, stirring. If the caramel solidifies, you've added the cream too quickly, in which case, just add all of the cream, reduce the heat to medium and stir for a while until the sugar melts into the cream. Once you have a smooth sauce, bring it to the boil for just a minute, then turn off the heat and add a pinch of salt flakes. Pour into a cold bowl and set aside until needed.

For the brownie batter, put the butter into a saucepan and set over a high heat. Allow the butter to sizzle and melt, swirling the pan every so often as it bubbles and spatters. Once the bubbles turn to a fine, cappuccino-like foam and the butter smells nutty, remove it from the heat.

Set a heatproof bowl over a pan of barely simmering water and add the chocolate to the bowl. Allow the chocolate to melt, then remove the bowl from the pan and add the browned butter, sugar and flour and beat until smooth. Add the eggs and beat until the mixture is extremely smooth and velvety.

Pour the mixture into the prepared cake tin and drizzle over 3 tablespoons of the salted caramel sauce. Scatter over half of the chopped hazelnuts. Bake for 30–35 minutes, until the brownie is puffed and set.

Unlike a properly baked cake, this will still be fairly fudgy inside, so the skewer test is redundant; instead I eat what comes out on the skewer and taste for starch. If the batter still tastes a little floury, bake it for a little longer until it just tastes chocolaty and rich. When the brownie is baked, allow it to cool in the tin for 15 minutes, then remove the brownie, still on the cake tin base, from the tin. Put into the fridge overnight, or the freezer for an hour or so. Once the brownie is firm, drizzle over more sauce, and scatter over the remaining hazelnuts. Cut into 16 equal pieces – a long chef's knife dipped into a tall jug of very hot water helps to slice the brownie neatly – just wipe the blade of the knife after each cut, and re-dip into the water. Serve immediately or store in an airtight tin for up to a week.

Plain Brownie

This recipe works to make a simple batch of plain brownies too. Simply omit the hazelnuts and salted caramel. Don't bother to brown the butter; just melt it with the chocolate in a bowl over a pan of simmering water, then continue as above. Because there's no caramel topping the brownie will be fully baked after 30 minutes. Don't forget to chill it before cutting.

something sweet

Marmalade on Toast & Tea Puddings

I'd imagine most people have memories of marmalade on toast with a mug of tea. Whenever I dunk my toast into the tea, that flavour just hurls me back to my childhood, sitting at the kitchen counter. These puddings perfectly embody that caressing combination.

Preheat the oven to 200°C/180°C fan/gas mark 6. Grease 4 × 180ml pudding moulds and line the bases with a disc of baking paper. Cut out 4 squares of baking paper slightly bigger than the top of the moulds and set aside.

First make a cup of tea: pour the boiling water over the tea bags in a mug and leave to infuse.

Toast the bread, and toast it well – the darker the toast, the better the flavour profile of the finished pudding. Blitz the bread to crumbs in a food processor or blender.

Put the butter and sugar in a mixing bowl and cream together until light and fluffy, then add the eggs, toast crumbs, cooled tea and flour. Mix to a smooth batter.

Put a tablespoon of the marmalade into each of the pudding moulds, then top with the pudding batter. Place a square of baking paper on top of the batter – don't press down or you'll compact the puddings. Transfer the moulds to a roasting tray and fill that with enough boiling water to come halfway up the sides of the moulds. Cover the tray with clingfilm, then with foil so that it is airtight, and bake the puddings for 30 minutes.

Remove the moulds carefully from the hot water and invert into individual serving dishes. Serve immediately – with lashings of cream, of course.

MAKES 4

100ml boiling water
2 English breakfast
  tea bags
150g sliced white bread
150g unsalted butter,
  at room temperature
100g light brown
  muscovado sugar
2 medium eggs
2 tbsp self-raising flour
4 tbsp Seville
  orange marmalade
Cream, to serve

Pecan, Cranberry & Dark Chocolate Pie

The deep treacly tones of classic pecan pie are perfect as they are, but I do think this version is hard to beat. Cranberries, with their subtle tang, and rich dark chocolate make the perfect foil against all the sweetness. I go a step further and first burn the butter to achieve a better depth of flavour, but you can just melt it if you prefer. I've given the ingredients for pastry here but you can always buy a 300g block of ready-made shortcrust pastry.

SERVES 8

For the pastry
125g unsalted butter, softened
50g caster sugar
1 medium egg
200g plain flour, plus extra for dusting
2g fine sea salt

For the filling
100g pecans
80g unsalted butter
1 tbsp golden syrup
1 tbsp treacle
100g light brown muscovado sugar
1 tbsp Bourbon whiskey
1 large egg
75g dried cranberries

For the ganache
75g dark chocolate, roughly chopped
100ml double cream

Preheat the oven to 200°C/180°C fan/gas mark 6.

For the pastry, cream the butter and sugar as though you were making a cake. Once the sugar has more or less dissolved into the butter, add the egg and beat in – don't worry if it curdles. Add the flour and salt and cut in using a dough scraper or butter knife. Once the mixture starts to clump together, briefly knead it until smooth. Flatten the pastry into a disc, wrap in clingfilm and chill for 30 minutes.

Meanwhile, scatter the pecans onto a baking tray and roast for 5–10 minutes in the oven, just until they dry out a little and start to release their sweet, nutty aroma. Remove the pecans from the oven and set aside until needed.

When the pastry has chilled, flour the worktop and roll the pastry out as thinly as you can manage without it becoming too delicate to handle. Lay the pastry into a 20cm fluted tart tin, ensuring you press it firmly into the grooves of the tin. Stab the base of the pastry repeatedly with a fork to ensure it doesn't balloon up while baking. Scrunch a sheet of baking paper into a ball, then unwrap it and lay it into the pastry case. Fill with baking beans or dried rice and blind-bake for 15 minutes. Remove the rice and paper, then bake for a further 15 minutes. Remove the tin from the oven and reduce the heat to 180°C/160°C fan/gas mark 4.

For the filling, put the butter into a small saucepan and set over a high heat. Allow the butter to sizzle and melt, swirling the pan every so often as it bubbles and spatters. Once the bubbles turn to a fine, cappuccino-like foam, and the butter smells nutty, remove the pan from the heat and add the syrup, treacle, brown sugar and Bourbon. Allow the mixture to cool slightly, before beating in the egg until you have a very smooth, velvety sauce.

Reserve 3 of the best looking pecans for the top and then scatter the rest into the base of the pastry case along with the cranberries. Carefully pour

the sauce over the top, leaving enough room for the chocolate ganache
layer, which comes later. Bake for 35–40 minutes, until the centre
of the pie is set but ever so slightly soft – prod it gently to find out.
Remove from the oven and allow to cool in the tin.

For the ganache, put the chocolate and cream into a heatproof bowl
and set over a pan of barely simmering water. Allow the chocolate to
melt into the cream, stirring occasionally, until you have a smooth,
glossy ganache. Pour the ganache over the tart, just until it threatens
to leak over the pastry wall. Dot the reserved pecans on top, and then
allow to set at room temperature until thick – a good hour or two.

The Lightest, Fluffiest Scones

These are the scones we make in the afternoon tea class at my cookery school, and they are the lightest, fluffiest beauties I've had. There's no real trickery to making them, just a process that most domestic scones recipes omit: resting the dough. This not only allows any gluten to relax and soften, but also it enables the baking powder to react, filling the dough with plenty of air. An important part is the working of the dough – it must be kneaded just until smooth, but take it any further and you'd risk the dough being tough and dense.

Half an hour or so before you start, put the buttermilk, crème fraîche and lemon juice into a jug and mix together. The mixture is intended to curdle, so don't throw it out. Leave to come to room temperature.

Put the flour into a mixing bowl with the baking powder, caster sugar and salt. Add the butter and rub together until the butter is evenly dispersed in the dry ingredients and the mixture resembles breadcrumbs. Add the wet ingredients into the bowl and start to mix – either with your hand or wooden spoon – until the mixture comes together into a scraggy mass. Tip the dough onto a lightly floured worktop and knead very briefly – no more than a minute or so – until it is smooth. The dough will be firm enough to hold its shape, but it will be tender and yielding to a poke. Put the dough onto a greased tray and cover with clingfilm. Leave to rest for 30 minutes.

Flour the worktop lightly and tip the dough onto it. Pat the dough down, with a floured hand, just until about 2cm thick – I don't bother with a rolling pin because the tendency is to over-roll it. Cut out using a 6cm(ish) cookie cutter. Set the scones on a greased tray, cover with clingfilm again, and leave to rest for a further 30 minutes.

Preheat the oven to 200°C/180°C fan/gas mark 6.

Once the scones have rested, flip them over so their flat bottoms become perfectly flat tops. If you put the scones fairly close together, with enough room in between each to allow for swelling, they will steam as they bake, keeping them softer. Glaze just the tops of the scones with the egg yolk, then bake for 12–15 minutes, until the tops are deeply golden and the bases are just gently browned. The scones will feel very soft, but they will firm up a little as they cool. Slide them onto a cooling rack and allow to cool, just until you can slather one liberally in cream and jam to eat without burning your mouth.

MAKES 10–12

150ml buttermilk
150g full-fat
   crème fraîche
Juice of ½ lemon
450g plain flour,
   plus extra for dusting
15g baking powder
80g caster sugar
Pinch of fine sea salt
80g unsalted butter,
   cubed, plus extra
   for greasing
1 large egg yolk, beaten
   with a pinch of salt

Cinnamon Buns

A couple of years ago, I impulsively booked a trip to Stockholm solely on the recommendation to visit one particular café – Café Saturnus. I'd heard tales of their cinnamon buns, perhaps the biggest and best in Sweden, and I wasn't disappointed. As big as my face, and as tender as you can imagine, the buns were beautiful. These aren't as big as the ones I ate in Stockholm, but they are just as delicious.

Despite the name, for an authentic flavour you actually need to include cardamom as well as cinnamon, but go carefully. I first used some ready-ground cardamom that I bought, and it must have been much softer than freshly ground cardamom from pods, because when I used those in the same quantity, they killed my poor yeast. So, learn from my mistake: if you grind your own pods, use just a quarter of the amount in the recipe.

MAKES 12

For the dough

250g plain flour

250g strong white
  bread flour

2 tsp ground cardamom
  (use ½ tsp if using
  freshly ground seeds
  from the pod)

10g caster sugar

5g salt

7g sachet fast-
  action yeast

150ml water, at
  room temperature

120ml milk, at
  room temperature

1 large egg

40g unsalted butter ▸

To make the dough, put the flours and cardamom into a bowl and stir in the sugar, salt and yeast. Add the water, milk and egg and mix well with a wooden spoon or your hands until you have a scraggy dough. Squeeze in the softened butter, then knead until the mixture is smooth and elastic – about 10 minutes by hand or 5 minutes in a mixer fitted with dough hook. The dough will be fairly sticky, but under no circumstances add any more flour – just keep at it and it will become tacky rather than sticky. Place the dough into an oiled bowl, cover with clingfilm and allow to rise until doubled in size – usually an hour but it could be quicker or slower, depending on the temperature of your kitchen.

To make the filling, beat together the butter, sugar, flour, cinnamon and cardamom until very paste-like – you will need to spread this onto the dough, so make sure it is very loose.

Preheat the oven to 220°C/200°C fan/gas mark 7.

Once the dough has doubled in size, lightly dust the worktop with flour and turn out the dough onto it. Roll the dough into a 45cm square and spread the filling over the dough as evenly as possible. Starting with the edge closest to you, fold one third of the dough over, then fold the top third over that first piece – just like folding a business letter. Roll briefly with a rolling pin to ensure all of the dough is stuck together. Trim the messy ends and discard them, then slice the dough into 12 slices. Take a slice of dough and twist gently until it starts to feel tight, then spiral it round itself and poke one end through the middle to form a knot. Repeat with the remaining pieces of dough, and place them, well-spaced, onto two lightly greased baking sheets. Allow to rest for another 20–30 minutes, or until they look slightly swollen.

Meanwhile put the caster sugar and water into a small saucepan and bring to the boil. Remove from the heat.

Bake the buns for 10 minutes until golden brown. Using a pastry brush, glaze the buns with the sugar syrup, as soon as they come out of the oven. Allow them to cool completely.

To finish the buns, beat together the icing sugar with enough lemon juice so the mixture has the consistency of golden syrup – you may need to add a drop or two of water to slacken it. Drizzle the icing over the buns and sprinkle with pearl sugar, if using.

For the filling
90g unsalted butter, softened, plus extra for greasing
70g light brown muscovado sugar
25g plain flour, plus extra for dusting
2 tbsp ground cinnamon
½ tsp ground cardamom (just use a pinch if using freshly ground seeds from the pod)

To finish
75g caster sugar
50ml water
100g icing sugar
1–2 tsp lemon juice
Pearl/nibbed sugar (optional)

something on the side

Self-preservation

We humans aren't too dissimilar to jams, chutneys and pickles. We can quite easily close ourselves off in order to take stock and develop as individuals. Like the quiet, gradual fizz of fermenting fruit, our profiles and characteristics change, sometimes for the better. But other times the result can be mouth-puckering, and we have to begin again. Perhaps we need a little stir or manipulation from something beyond our control. It's a waiting game, until we ultimately discover the best version of ourselves.

These are the thoughts that consume me as I stir pots – the process, like fishing, is well suited to deep thinkers. Great vats of damson jam and single jars of pickles invoke in me a feeling of self-preservation, a survival, albeit without pain (apart from the odd spurt of hot jam escaping from the pan, always landing on the most tender parts of my forearms or knuckles).

What I like most is how this preserving process isn't just restorative, but how it reconnects us with nature too: we take from our gardens, hedgerows and orchards such bountiful nourishment, which can be squirrelled away for colder times. Jam making is a sort of paradox: we reconnect to feel alive, yet we withdraw to regenerate.

Preparing to Pickle
When making jams, chutneys or anything that you are storing in a glass jar, it's important the jar is sterilised.

To sterilise your jars (don't forget the lids and the ladle), either run them through a hot cycle in the dishwasher, or scrub with hot soapy water before drying in an oven preheated to 140°C/120°C fan/ gas mark 1 for 30 minutes. Once they are sterilised, don't even think about touching the inside of either jar or lid.

Label your jars, or you may regret it. After a heavy night out I once hauled myself into the kitchen for jam on toast. I ended up with fiery Christmas chutney on my bread: a sobering mistake.

Damson, Guinness & Cocoa Jam

Every year I make a batch or two of damson jam. Out of all the jams, this is one of the most involved processes; removing the stones is the most patience-testing part, but really it's just a case of skimming them away with a slotted spoon as the fruit breaks down. They lurk just beneath the surface like sharks in a blood-red pool, so be sure not to miss any. When I was little, my grandfather used to give me jam and cottage cheese on toast as a bedtime snack. This jam makes for a version of that treat that I am sure he would have loved.

MAKES 6–8 300g JARS

First sterilise your jam jars and lids (see page 210).

1.3kg damsons
1 x 440ml can Guinness
1.5kg caster sugar
4 tbsp cocoa powder

Put the damsons and Guinness into a large saucepan and set over a high heat. Stir while the contents of the pan come to the boil, then reduce to a brisk simmer and cook, stirring occasionally, until the fruit has completely broken down. It's tempting to skip this part, but – trust me – it'll make your life easier when it comes to skimming out the stones

Add the sugar to the pan and stir to dissolve. The stones (and some skins) will float to the surface. Remove the stones with a slotted spoon.

Sift the cocoa powder into a small bowl and stir together with enough of the damson liquid to create a thick paste. Pour the paste into the jam pan and stir to incorporate.

Bring the jam to the boil and cook, stirring occasionally, until it reaches 105°C on a digital thermometer – stir the jam before you take the temperature reading.

Ladle the hot jam into the sterilised jars and screw on the lids. Label and store in a cool place.

Out of Season?
If it isn't damson season, but you have the urge to make something similar, try using an equal mixture of frozen blackcurrants and blackberries instead.

Rhubarb, Ginger & Campari Jam

This is a fabulous jam. The flavour profile changes with every bite: at first you get that sweet tang of rhubarb, which slowly transforms into a warm spice from the ginger. As that fades you're left with the bitter hit of the Campari.

First sterilise your jam jars and lids (see page 210).

Trim the rhubarb, cut into small chunks and add to a large pan with the remaining ingredients. Bring to the boil and cook down until a digital thermometer reads 105°C. This will take a while because the water content from both rhubarb and Campari will need to evaporate – make sure you stir the jam very frequently to prevent it from burning on the bottom, and stir before you take the temperature reading.

Ladle the hot jam into the sterilised jars and screw on the lids. Label and store in a cool place.

MAKES 6–8 300g JARS

1.5kg rhubarb
1.5kg caster sugar
40g fresh ginger,
  peeled and
  finely chopped
Juice of 1 lemon
250ml Campari

something on the side

Coleslaw, Four Ways

Food is bloody difficult – even condiments are points of great contention. Coleslaw divides so many – some like it with onion, others without; some like it sweet, others prefer it sour and slightly hot. These recipes are just a few of the many I make that have come to be firm favourites.

I like to macerate my vegetables first in sugar and salt – a process which draws out water, leaving a deeper taste. The texture changes too. It becomes softer, but somehow retains crunch, which is delicious. It may seem like a lot of salt and sugar, but most of it dissolves in the liquid from the veg, which in any case gets discarded.

Use a mandolin to finely slice the cabbage and onion and put into a bowl with the grated carrots. Sprinkle over the salt and sugar, cover with clingfilm and leave for an hour or so.

After this brief stint the salt and sugar will have drawn out an incredible amount of moisture. Put the vegetables into a sieve and rinse under cold water, then squeeze out all of the moisture. The vegetables will have become a little limp, but should still retain a soft crunch.

Put the vegetables into a bowl with the remaining ingredients and stir until well combined.

The coleslaw will keep in a sterilised jar in the fridge for 5 days or so, but is much better fresh.

MAKES ABOUT 500g

200g red cabbage,
  without the core
1 medium red onion
200g purple carrots,
  coarsely grated
2 tbsp sea salt flakes
75g caster sugar
1 tbsp red wine vinegar
3 tbsp mayonnaise
1 tbsp soured cream

Variations

Fennel and Orange
Replace 100g of the cabbage with 100g finely sliced fennel bulb and continue as above. Add the juice and zest of $1/2$ orange, along with 2 teaspoons fennel seeds, toasted in a hot pan for no more than a minute.

Sunflower Seed and Dill
Toast 75g sunflower seeds in a hot pan for a minute or so, tossing frequently, until browned. Add to the recipe above with 1 tablespoon finely chopped fresh dill fronds.

Waldorf
Add 75g roughly chopped walnuts and 75g chopped dried apple to the recipe above. And if you have any, use apple cider vinegar in place of the red wine vinegar.

Pickled Orange Fennel

So many people turn their nose up at fennel, disliking its slight aniseed flavour. But for me that's something to behold. Its faint anise notes, and sweet, crunchy texture are just gorgeous. Pickled like this, fennel's flavour is amplified, and its crispness softens to a more tender bite. Serve with steamed salmon and veg, or simply with cold cuts of meats.

ENOUGH FOR A 340G JAR

2 small fennel bulbs,
  long stalks removed
  (reserve the fronds)
2 tsp sea salt flakes
2 tsp caster sugar
1 tbsp fresh dill fronds,
  roughly chopped

For the pickling liquor
225ml white wine vinegar
100ml water
3 tbsp caster sugar
1 tsp yellow
  mustard seeds
1 tsp dried chilli flakes
1 tsp nigella seeds
Zest of 2 unwaxed
  oranges

First sterilise your jam jar and lid (see page 210).

Slice the fennel into very thin strips – either by hand, cutting the bulb in half, then placing it cut-side down on a chopping board, while you shave ultra-thin slices with a knife, or with a mandolin. Rinse the fennel well, tip into a bowl, sprinkle over the salt and sugar and toss together. Leave, covered with clingfilm, to macerate for an hour.

When the fennel has released plenty of liquid, drain it well and pack it into the sterilised jar with the reserved fennel and dill fronds.

Put the ingredients for the pickling liquor into a small saucepan and stir to dissolve the sugar. Bring the mixture to the boil, then allow it to bubble for a minute. Pour the pickling liquid over the fennel. Allow to cool, seal with the lid and refrigerate. This is best eaten after about a week – or longer if you can bear.

It will keep for a few months in the fridge.

Anise & Bay Pickled Radishes

Radishes just aren't what they used to be. I remember at primary school – I was in year 4 – the husband of one of the teaching assistants, who was also in charge of our allotment, gave me my first radish. He plucked a flick knife from his flannel shirt pocket, rinsed the radish under the tap in the trough sink in between the classrooms, sliced it in half and gave it to me. My immature palate couldn't take it. In fact, I think I spat it on the floor. It was wild and fiery, like nothing I'd had before, except, perhaps, a lick of horseradish from my mother's steak knife when she'd turned her head. Nowadays, as with most fruit and veg, the flavour of radishes seems to have been dulled – I don't know whether it's over-farming – but I guarantee that pickling helps to reinstate their former peppery glory.

First sterilise your jam jar and lid (see page 210).

Slice the radishes as finely as you can manage – preferably with a mandolin. Put them into a bowl and sprinkle over the 2 tablespoons salt and sugar. Cover with clingfilm and leave to macerate for at least an hour. After this time, put the radishes into a sieve and rinse under the cold tap to remove all the salt and sugar, then pack them into the sterilised jar.

Put the ingredients for the pickling liquor into a small saucepan and stir to dissolve the sugar. Bring the mixture to the boil then pour it over the radishes. Allow to cool then seal with the lid and refrigerate. These can be used right away but are best after about a week.

These will keep for a few months in the fridge.

ENOUGH FOR A 340G JAR

200g radishes
2 tbsp sea salt flakes
2 tbsp caster sugar

For the pickling liquor
200g red wine vinegar
4 tbsp caster sugar
1 bay leaf
1 star anise

Toasted Pumpkin Seed
& Parsley Pesto

This is a pesto with a lot more depth than the regular basil and pine nut version. The toasted pumpkin seeds echo strongly through the pesto; the result is something a little more autumnal in flavour.

MAKES 1 JAR

80g pumpkin seeds
60g flat-leaf parsley
225ml extra virgin
   olive oil (I like to use
   Ligurian), plus extra
   for topping up the jar
100g pecorino cheese,
   coarsely grated
Juice of ½ lemon
1 tsp sea salt flakes

First sterilise the jam jar and lid (see page 210).

Heat a dry frying pan over a high heat and add the pumpkin seeds. Shake the pan every so often and allow the seeds to toast – they will crackle and pop like popcorn. Once the popping subsides, put the seeds into a food processor with the remaining ingredients. Blitz to a coarse paste.

Pack the paste into the sterilised jar and top with a layer of oil to ensure it is airtight. Keep in the fridge for up to a week – though it may last a little longer. Every time you use a bit, just ensure there's a thin layer of oil on top of the pesto before popping it back in the fridge.

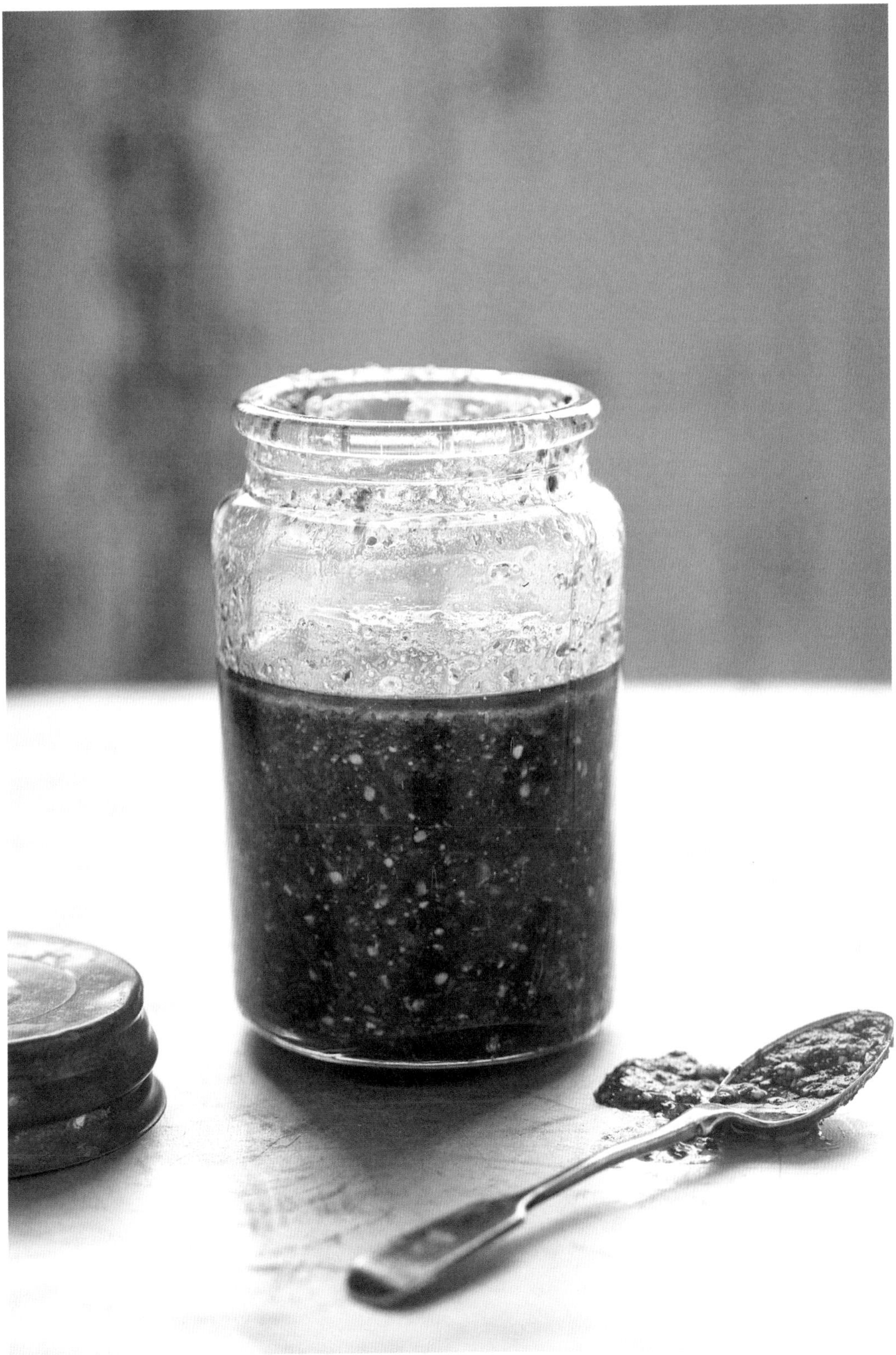

Index

Index

To my companions, with thanks

My favourite form of comfort, apart from the edible kind, is companionship. It's easy to take for granted the people with whom we share moments, experiences or lifetimes.

To everyone who worked on this book, from the very first meeting, to the final photograph, thank you for creating memories, and thank you for the companionship.

John Whaite won the third series of the BBC's *The Great British Bake Off*. He studied at the Le Cordon Bleu, though his love of food came from learning at his mother's knee and growing up as a farmer's son. He is resident chef on ITV's Lorraine. He has his own cookery school, John Whaite's Kitchen. This is his fourth book.